The Bear Guarding the Beehive

The Bear Guarding the Beehive

Stephanie C. Fox, J.D.

QueenBeeBooks

Bloomfield, Connecticut, U.S.A.

Library of Congress Cataloging-in-Publication Data
Name: Fox, Stephanie C., author.
Title: The Bear Guarding the Beehive / Stephanie C. Fox.
Description: Connecticut: QueenBeeBooks, [2014].
Includes bibliographical references.
Identifiers: ISBN 978-0-9996395-4-2 (paperback)
Subjects: 1. Environmental—Law. 2. Ecosystems &
Habitats – General—Nature. 3. Public Policy – Agriculture
& Food Policy (see also Agriculture & Food—Social
Science)—Political Science.

www.queenbeeedit.com

Cover design by Stephanie C. Fox
Cover art by Lauren Jane Leipold
Printed in the United States of America

This story is dedicated to honey bees, beekeepers, and independent scientists.

Also by Stephanie C. Fox

The Book of Thieves

Nae-Née
Birth Control: Infallible, with
Nanites and Convenience for All

Vaccine: The Cull
Nae-Née Wasn't Enough

New World Order Underwater
The Nae-Née Inventors Strike Back

What the Small Gray Visitor Said

Intrigue On a Longship Cruise

Elephant's Kitchen
– An Aspergirl's Study in Difference

Almost a Meal –
A True Tale of Horror

Scheherazade Cat:
The Story of a War Hero

An American Woman in Kuwait

Hawai'i – Stolen Paradise:
A Travelogue

Hawai'i – Stolen Paradise:
A Brief History

FPPL CJP QNLCDDPCJNEK CEQ SP
BEES ARE DISAPPEARING AND WE

QRE'H YERS SOY.
DON'T KNOW WHY.

HONL NL C LPJNRXL TCHHPJ – NH CZZPUHL
THIS IS A SERIOUS MATTER—IT AFFECTS

RXJ ZRRQ LXDDGV.
OUR FOOD SUPPLY.

HSR-HONJQL RZ RXJ ZJXNHL CEQ BPKKNPL
TWO-THIRDS OF OUR FRUITS AND VEGGIES

CJP DRGGNECHPQ FV C FPP,
ARE POLLINATED BY A BEE,

LR SP OCBP HR LRGBP HONL DJRFGPT – N
SO WE HAVE TO SOLVE THIS PROBLEM—I

HONEY VRX SNGG CKJPP.
THINK YOU WILL AGREE.

— By Nancy Eisenmann

*"That which is not good for the bee-hive
cannot be good for the bees."*
- Marcus Aurelius

*"Swallows have disappeared,
bees are dying out
because of pesticides that
should have been banned
long ago – it's a scandal."*
- Brigitte Bardot

Table of Contents

A Conflict of Interest

Entrusting our environment and its safety and integrity to chemicals, and stressing the elements that keep us healthy to the brink of extinction, is like leaving the bear guarding the beehive.

Soon you will know why – and in detail – our planet cannot grow enough food to sustain human life, or other life as it we know and love it.

The basic cause is a conflict of interest.

Imagine a bear guarding a beehive.

Bears love honey, but if they can take it all, they will. If a beehive loses all of its honey, it must start over. It will need a new queen bee, new honeycomb, new stores of beeswax to hold new honey – everything must be redone from scratch.

So what? A hive can start over...but at what cost?

But what if there are bears everywhere, unchecked, doing this to most of the hives rather than just a few? Bears preventing the bees from doing what they need to do undisturbed, bears grabbing all that they can get their paws on, bears preventing others from having access?

When you have a bear guarding the beehive, there will never be enough honey or enough healthy bees to pollinate the plants that other life forms need to survive. Without healthy, undisturbed bees to pollinate and collect nectar from those plants – flowers and flowering food plants such as fruits and nuts – the natural world that is our environment will collapse.

We don't want that to happen.

Habitat loss, diseases introduced from too much travel, exhaustion from that same overextension of bees' immune systems, a diet of empty calories, poisons being released where bees forage, and general use and abuse had induced stressors that comprised a perfect storm, whipped up against the bees.

I will tell you about the conflict of interest that drove it all, one between money and Nature.

This is the story of what happened with bees in the nation of Oblivion.

It all happened while the people of Oblivion were going about their business, determined to grow more and more fruits and nuts to support their ever-growing human population. This population assumed that it could grow and grow endlessly; that the natural world could be manipulated to support human needs…and wants.

It couldn't, and it still can't.

That is not something that the Oblivious wanted to face, however.

The people of Oblivion were absolutely determined to ignore this reality, and to coax – and force – more and more and more from their land. They thought that this could go on indefinitely, and monster corporations were allowed to form with this end in mind.

Of course, huge sums of money were involved.

One of them specialized in killing off the insects that eat fruits, vegetables, and other plants that humans grow for food. The owners of this monster corporation thought they were very clever, but they were not. I will tell you why.

When you aim to kill off some insects, you cannot pick and choose which ones.

A poison, once released into the environment, kills whatever insect it comes into contact with, regardless of whether or not that insect interferes or assists with food production or other plant growth. Once released, a chemical stays in the soil permanently. It adheres to whatever plant it comes in contact with, affecting the plant's molecular structure as it grows.

This affects any other insect that touches it, like the honey bee. It also affects any human who eats the food of that plant, harming the health of that individual. Sometimes the wiser course is to leave Nature alone, but the Oblivious were not wise people.

I will tell you why toxic chemicals were being released into the environment and killing the honey bees. I will tell you what else was killing the honey bees, because it was not only toxins. It won't be pleasant.

Beauty and the Bees

We have a lot to thank the honey bees for.

If only the people of Oblivion had thought of that sooner!

But...we humans are a foolish and short-sighted species.

We have wonderful gifts that we don't appreciate or protect: a beautiful planet with blue skies, breathable air, sunshine, plants that feed us and have lovely scents and appearances, crucial insects that we call honey bees (and other bees, such as bumblebees), talent, ingenuity, and the physical ability to take care of it all and enjoy it.

Yet most of us don't do that. Too few of us do that to really make a difference.

Why?!

Not enough of us read and take the initiative to learn the consequences of using poisons on our natural environment and to identify safe, viable alternatives. As a result, not enough of us protest the rampant application of poison to our habitat, which is insane when you recall that this planet is the only one that we've got. We can't just move to another one, because there isn't one.

As life evolved on our planet, it adapted to poisons by developing where those poisons – such as arsenic, radioactive elements, and other mutagens – did not exist. Yet now we unleash these toxins upon Nature, all the while expecting the aspects of it that we like and that have benefitted us for eons to remain unchanged. This is insane. It simply does not work.

The world that honey bees makes possible is the most beautiful, wonderful, amazing array of sights, scents, and tastes that we could hope for. (It should be noted that other insects and some birds play a significant role in pollination, but our focus is on the bees. All are threatened by human shortsightedness, greed and stupidity, but this is not an entomology treatise. This is a plea to protect the honey bees, and so I shall concentrate on them.)

This planet grows raspberries, strawberries, blackberries, blueberries, oranges, apples, apricots, peaches, almonds – yes, nuts! – to eat, all due to the industry of honey bees, whose honey takes on a different color and flavor depending upon which fruit the bees have pollinated.

And that's not all. The world has gorgeous flowers of all kinds: every iris, peony, rose, lavender, daffodil, Rose of Sharon, hibiscus, foxgloves, and many others…this list could go on and on and on. Huge numbers of them are pollinated by bees.

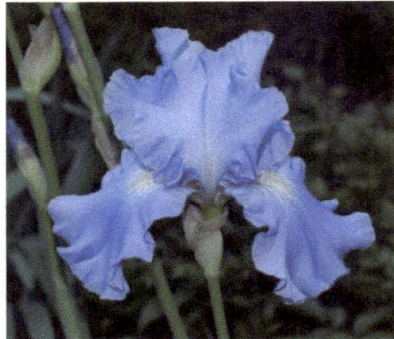

Pollen-bearing flowers: pastel pink peony at left,
tall bearded pale blue iris at right.

5

Some are pollinated by birds. Hummingbirds pollinate bee balm, ironically enough! They also do that for bird-of-paradise. Still others, such as plumeria, are pollinated by moths and butterflies.

Regardless, flowers are wonderful. Enough of them are made possible by bees that one would expect that human behavior ought to protect them.

It doesn't.

Life without this amazing beauty and these alluring scents would be very different, and we would feel the lack keenly if faced with it.

They make life worth living because they keep us healthy, both physically and mentally.

We need fruits to eat. Humans get sick with scurvy and other forms of malnutrition without fruits. Those of us who eat birds and animals would have a problem without the bees, because the bees enable foods that those creatures eat to grow.

Raspberry Blueberry Tart, with fruit pollinated by bees.

We need flowers because flowers grow in tandem with fruit plants – they are part of them. Flowers are the tease that lures the honey bees over to the fruit plants. The bee pollinates the flowers on a raspberry vine, for example, and as a result the raspberries grow. No honey bees, no raspberries! This is true of all of the fruit plants that we humans depend upon for survival.

The other flowers – the ones that we grow for pleasure in our gardens, and that perfumers use to make the fragrances that so many of us enjoy using – are also pollinated by bees.

Life without the honey bees would be very bleak.

It would not include chocolate, coffee, vanilla, pumpkins, melons, or berries.

It would also end for us in just a few years, because without the honey bees – without the fruits, nuts, and vegetables that they enable to grow – we humans would die.

But…we humans are foolish.

We wait until a crisis is upon us to change our behavior, and that means that we wait far too long. By the time we have no bees, it will be too late.

That is why I am writing this story: I intend to do something before that happens, not after.

Healthy Honey Bees – An Illustration in Words

Healthy honey bees produce healthy food and make anyone who eats it healthy.

This should not seem like a difficult concept, but it was in Oblivion.

People in Oblivion did not pay close attention to how their food was produced and insist upon safe growing, harvesting, or production methods for much of their history. That is not wise, logical, or thoughtful, but that is how it was.

Thus, it seems like a good idea to provide a brief illustration in words of how things ought to be for the honey bees and for humans. It helps to understand what is wrong with a picture if one knows how things look when all is as it ought to be.

Communing with the Honey Bees

A beekeeper and her honey bees live life with no guarantees but plenty of satisfaction.

At least, that is the case as long as the environment – the ecosystem in which they exist – is healthy, uncontaminated by toxins, and functioning as it should.

She is constantly busy and concerned with her bees, giving them whatever they need, watching them, making sure that they are comfortable, busy, healthy, and producing honey. This is her life throughout each season of each year. She longs to be with the bees, but she is determined not to let that feeling cause her to disturb the bees too early.

Autumn, winter, spring, and summer, her thoughts are first and foremost of her bees.

In the autumn, she might sell some hives to a new beekeeper. It is the start of a new year for the bees, a time when they are getting ready for winter. Of course, this is only true if the beekeeper has no intention of pushing the bees to produce honey or do any pollinating work on any schedule other than their own. That is what I am describing here: the life of a beekeeper who communes with the bees rather than one who uses them for whatever she can get.

Whatever honey a new beekeeper reaps from a hive is not known until it appears, available to a human taker, not needed by the hive as food to survive the winter.

Bees survive winter at the lower center of their hive, close together, moving constantly to keep warm. A cluster of honey bees moves around the hive during the winter, staying together as it eats the honey that has been stored until the weather warms up, and then they are ready to go out and gather pollen and nectar to rebuild the hive's supply.

During the winter, the beekeeper checks her supplies, making sure that she has everything in perfect order for the spring. She will need frames for her hives for when they swarm, because when they do, the hive doubles in size and needs a new home. She intends to have it ready.

Langstroth Beehives, designed by Lorenzo Langstroth in 1851.

Her beehives are made of wood – pine – and are often, but not always, box-shaped. These boxes are piled one on top of the other until there are two or three of them, in a tall rectangle; small apian skyscrapers. However, and I shall explain that more later on, there are other shapes.

Humans have sought honey on every continent for millennia, but only in the past century and a half did we begin to construct hives for the bees. Bees will move into them, but they are also perfectly capable of constructing their own hives. It should be noted that apian architecture is drastically different from human efforts, and the human beekeeper of almost two centuries ago designed his hives with human convenience and efficiency in mind.

Each pine box contains ten frames. Nine of them are for the bees to live in; the tenth is a feeder, which the beekeeper pours liquid into. This liquid is sugar syrup. This is food for the bees, to consume when they need more than they can manage to gather during warm weather. The beekeeper does not take honey from this box, called the hive body.

Inside a Langstroth hive: 9 frames and a feeder panel, for sugar water.

Over the hive body, she puts a screen that is called a queen excluder.

A queen excluder is exactly what it sounds like: it keeps the queen, who is a larger insect than the other bees in the hive, from leaving the hive body. Thus confined, she can only lay eggs – called pupae – in that section.

View inside a Langstroth hive with a queen excluder in place.

You guessed it; there is another section of the hive that goes over this. It is called a super, and it is half as tall as the hive body. This is where the beekeeper takes honey from. She may stack two or more of these supers on top of the hive body. Other than the depth, the design of the supers matches that of the hive body.

A super over a queen excluder, with frames of honey and comb.

Each frame is made of pine slats that fit together, with sheets of wax and wire crossed around and melted through the wax. The wax foundation is sold in sheets, and must be handled in a warm room, or it will break. This foundation is shaped with a hexagonal pattern. All of these 6-sided holes are for the bees to live in, breed in, work in, and store honey in. Because they are machine-made and ordered shipped to each beekeeper, each hexagon is the same size. More on this later; size matters.

A frame from a super, partially covered with honeycomb, on machine-made hexagonal cells.

In the land of Oblivion, beekeepers usually paint their hives white, but those who have traveled south, to the neighboring nation, have seen a rainbow of colors on hives. There are no rules about what color to use.

When spring comes, the beekeeper checks the hives to see how the bees have fared over the cold season. She puts on her loose white suit, zipping herself into it so that no bees can get inside as she works, and tops it off with a veiled hat, also zipped to the rest of her outfit.

A beekeeper hat with veil attached.

Finally, she brings her smoker, a large, metal can with a conical, angled spout and a pump-fan on the side. The fuel can be discarded fabric, which must be made of natural cotton fibers, but dried grass, leaves, needles from fir trees, and other natural compost from the forest floor are good, too.

A beekeeper preparing a smoker with pine needles as fuel.

The purpose of the smoker is to calm the bees. She releases the smoke outside the hive once it is burning steadily and cool; hot, sparking smoke would burn the bees. All this preparation is to prevent being stung, but the truth is that beekeepers do get stung, and they build up immunity to bee venom. They train their apprentices with a sting at a time as well, just to make sure that each one can tolerate the venom, as not everyone can.

Smokers, seen from the side and back, puffing smoldering cotton and pine needles.

The venom in a bee sting marks a human as a hostile intruder who intends to steal the hive's honey, so of course the beekeeper needs a good smoker. Once the bees are in a calm stupor, she can raid the hive of honey without being tagged with pheromones, which make up the marker in the bee venom.

Some beekeepers claim that bee venom soothes arthritis, a degeneration of the joints that causes pain as bones rub against one another. Scientists are still working to prove this, but that is just another positive reason to save the bees. The mere possibility makes the idea very attractive.

The beekeeper doesn't just come prepared with a suit and a smoker. She also brings a frame grip and a short, wide tool like a crowbar. She uses these items to pry the hive apart, because the bees have sealed themselves in for the winter, and another tool called a frame grip, to pick up each frame as she checks on them. She wants to make sure that they are alive and well, and that they have a healthy queen. She makes sure that they still have enough reserves in the feeder, too.

Hive tools and a frame gripper.

Once she is satisfied that this is the case, she returns to her role as observer. She checks on her honey bees constantly, finding it relaxing and fun. She does not feel that they owe her anything. She has chosen to keep bees; they had nothing to do with this decision.

She wanders the area around her hives, checking to see what blooms first, always with its usefulness to her bees in mind. Whatever the bees pollinate most flavors their honey. Some people in Oblivion love orange blossom honey best; others love clover honey, still others blackberry, raspberry, or blueberry honey.

About the honey bees themselves…what is life like from their point of view?

Bees can't hear.

Bees can see every color but red – blue, violet, green, yellow, white.

They aren't as interested in yellow and white, but will go to flowers of those hues if they see no other colors. Why? There are plenty of other insects that focus exclusively on yellow and white blossoms.

Did you know that there are several kinds of bees in each hive, and that most are female?

It's true.

There is the queen bee, of course, whose entire life is devoted to laying eggs.

The majority of the hive is made up of infertile females. They are called worker bees, and they have a variety of jobs. There are nurse bees, scout bees, attendant bees…they all have different but necessary tasks to perform.

Attendant bees take care of the queen bee's every physical need, feeding and cleaning her, following her around constantly so that she need do absolutely nothing but lay eggs and seal them into their own hexagonal cells. Nurse bees take care of the pupae until they are fully grown, new bees crawling out to join the hive.

A queen bee, worker bees, and pupae on a hive frame.

16

Scout bees look for nectar and pollen to store and eat, and for propolis, which is a resinous mixture from tree sap and other sources. Bees use propolis for sealing off the hive against mites, intruders, and decaying intruders that have somehow gotten in and then died. Scouts also look for new places for a swarming hive to move to.

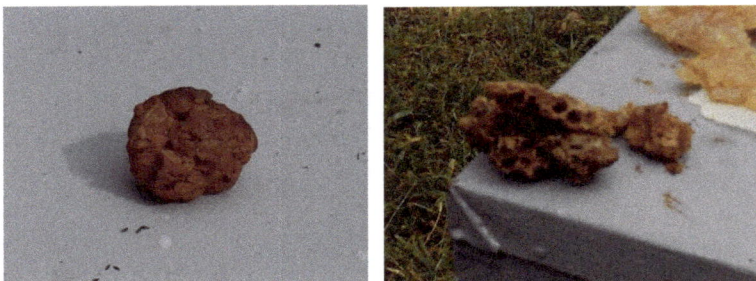

Propolis at left, used by bees for sealing hives against invaders of all kinds and for its anti-bacterial properties, and honeycomb at right, used by beekeepers to make beeswax products, including candles and soap.

When a scout bee has found whatever is required, she returns to the hive and does a dance. Each step is a part of a map: so many buzzes north, then turn east for a bit, then land at the destination, or something like that. Other workers go and gather nectar and pollen, and bring it back to the hive. If there are enough workers doing one job, a few will sense this and go do something else.

No worker bee spends more than three and a half hours per day actually doing work. For several hours, she will patrol the hive, just checking to see that everything is okay, and the rest of the time she will rest in a hexagonal cell, doing nothing. Rest is good.

What a comparison to a human cubicle worker! Humans in Oblivion have been known to refer to themselves as "worker bees" after these amazing insects, and derive a lot less happiness and satisfaction from their efforts. They work a lot more, and get a lot less…but that is another story, one that is told in another book.

Bees have a hive mind, but they are also individuals. They communicate very rapidly and effectively. A beekeeper does not need to interfere in order for the bees to function. The wise ones just watch and learn, and only make a move when they see that the bees need something.

What about the males?

They are called drones. They lead very short lives. They are born to mate with the queen, and they die right after they do so. The more drones the queen can mate with on her first and only flight outside of the hive, the better.

She must store the genetic material she acquires for the rest of her life, because that is what she will use to create more bees. Queen bees live for two or three years, longer than any other bees in the hive.

A drone, left, and a female worker bee with a drone, right.

Sometimes, a beekeeper will see that the bees need a new hive, so she will put out empty ones, ready for them to move into. This is in her interest; she wants the honey to eat and to sell. That is how she keeps herself in the beekeeping business, after all. When they swarm, they leave the hive en masse – in a noisy group, moving and swirling together as they seek out a new home.

Many people find this alarming, because they have convinced themselves that swarming bees will attack them. This is not so. Swarming bees won't bother them. Leave a bee alone, and it will leave you alone. Just watch and see what it does, and don't bother the bees! This is known as respecting Nature, which is very powerful. Powerful forces can hurt you if you don't leave them alone, but they can benefit you if you learn about them and stay out of their way.

A beekeeper who has prepared for swarming can split her hives, much like a cell dividing and becoming two complete, functioning cells. But on occasion, someone else will want to buy a hive. For that, the beekeeper will nail the hive levels together, and seal the exit, which is in the front at the bottom, with a moving screen. Once the hive is in its new spot, preferably at the north end of a clearing facing south, this can be removed.

Do you know what bees gather, what they use it for, and what they produce?

It's not all about honey, despite their name. They also produce royal jelly and beeswax.

Nurse bees use royal jelly to grow new bees. To grow new queen bees, they simply surround some larvae with it, and feed them extra royal jelly. The nurse bees feed all larvae royal jelly, but up the allotment considerably on some of them when their queen is getting near the end of her reproductive life so that a pool of replacement candidates will become available. The replacements try to kill each other at birth; the winner becomes the new queen bee.

Pupae, pollen, and nurse bees.

Beeswax is used to seal honey into the hive frames; without it, the honey would ooze away. It is also used to seal individual hexagonal pupae cells off from one another. That is why the beekeeper uses her hive tool to break the frames apart from one another in the spring.

A healthy frame of brood and bees.

Earlier, I mentioned that hives are constructed differently when humans are not involved.

Have you ever seen a children's book with illustrations that depict natural beehives? The hives look like tall mounds – humps – with a small exit at the bottom that resembles the frame of a curved door. Except that there is no door, at least not in the summertime.

Some humans have studied this, with a view toward considering the needs and purposes of the bees rather than their own. Here is what they have noticed: the hexagonal cells in a natural beehive are not all the same size! They are of graduated sizes, from smallest deep inside the hive to medium to largest on the outside.

Natural honeycomb, built up over a period of 3 months.

Why? The reason seems to be that it is easiest to clean cells of mites and other undesirable material if they are near the perimeter, and toughest if they are in the interior. Having smaller cells solves this problem because they leave no room for intruders. As a result, some beekeepers have been building hives with panels that are tapered toward the bottom, with varying cell sizes.

Humans have a lot more to learn from Nature. We should keep observing it.

But back to honey. Honey must be eaten raw to give its promised boost to the human immune system, not simply stirred into hot tea, which kills it. Honey is the one food that never rots, and thus keeps on the shelf indefinitely. Honey is better than cough and cold medicines.

Honey contains something called glycogen, which is brain food. Without it, brain cells die. Without it, a stress hormone called cortisol is produced. Cortisol causes all sorts of damage: in large amounts, it causes obesity – severe weight gain. With glycogen, humans can avoid diabetes and heart trouble, and with stress better. In ancient times, humans even used honey as a wound dressing.

Whether or not we realize it, we all commune with the honey bees.

Several Langstroth beehives, and at left, a top-bar hive.

They keep us alive and well.

This is a true story, one that may save your life if you learn it well, so pay attention, and heed the warnings that were ignored by the people of Oblivion.

In Memoriam to the Bees

If you want to know what killed the bees, read on.

But be prepared for a sickening sense of anxiety and regret for what was.

It's the least you can do for the bees.

If only more had been done sooner, we would still have honey, raspberries, and health.

But that's gone now.

Pestituted

Oblivion suffered from an endemic problem: Thieves.

Thieves infested it like mites, mold, poison, and other toxins.

The Thieves of the land of Oblivion were many: they owned and operated big banks and huge corporations. They bought and paid for the services of corrupt politicians and Pressure-Pointers – attorneys who spoke for them – and smaller players in the same morass of greed that plagued Oblivion. The Thieves all depended on one another in some way, be it through money or influence or both, to steal successfully.

When these guys weren't busy stealing and hatching new plots with which to steal, they arranged private parties. Some of these parties included cocktails and poets. Other parties included huge sporting events with private rooms at the top of the arena from which to watch in great luxury while eating grand buffets catered by gourmet restaurants. Still others involved exclusive nightclubs with prostitutes.

That last bit was the ironic part, because the Thieves were all prostituted to one another.

Beekeepers and scientists, who knew about these parties, had another term for the Thieves who worked in the agribusiness and chemical industries: Pestitutes.

The reason for this term is that, instead of calling their products insecticides, which is what they really were, the Thieves called them pesticides. Because the agribusiness and chemical industries wanted to kill insects, they called insects "pests" rather than insects, as if every species were an unwanted nuisance. They did so while ignoring the fact that one could not use the products and also pick and choose which insects would be affected by them.

The Thieves had no understanding of Nature, nor any respect for its awesome forces.

All they cared about was making more and more and more money, even if that money came from a temporary source that destroyed the planet's capability to grow life-sustaining foods. The next generation of humans could worry about that, the Thieves assumed.

At this point, it should be added that the Thieves were not deep thinkers, as it never seemed to occur to them that the next generation of humans would include their own descendants.

BearGenics and Natural Manipulators

There were two huge corporations in the land of Oblivion. They were swollen with money, with the Thieves who ran them, and with arrogance toward Nature. They had too much money and too little wisdom. They bought knowledge with their money, and used in any way that enabled them to increase profits. The money enabled the Thieves to make selfish, short-sighted decisions.

This was a huge problem for the honey bees.

The names of these corporations were BearGenics and Natural Manipulators.

BearGenics and Natural Manipulators each had corporate offices in the state of Dementia, which had the friendliest laws in all of Oblivion to corporations.

BearGenics specialized in supplying seeds to big agribusinesses. An agribusiness was yet another variety of monstrous corporation, one that used agriculture as a means of mass producing food, including corn, wheat, soy, sunflowers, almonds, and anything else that could be grown on large stretches of land. These were huge farms, run like corporations, with their owners both physically and emotionally distanced from the land and crops that they oversaw.

There were still farms run by independent families, but the agribusinesses had teamed up with BearGenics. They were all determined to own Oblivion's food supply and run the farmers out of the food production industry.

What an odd term: the food production industry.

What Nature enables people to produce, either in a home garden, on a city rooftop or plot, on a farm in the countryside, or on vast acres owned by a soulless corporation, is supposed to be food that is safe to eat. It is not supposed to be an industrial operation, like a factory.

It should be all natural, grown without anything artificial or poisonous, and not in a hurry. It should taste wonderful, as it still does when grown without those things. The term for such a growing method is "organic." Some grocery stores did offer such foods.

It was strange that a special effort had to be made. It was one thing to go to a farmers' market in the summer and fall to buy things that were produced locally and did in fact taste wonderful, with nothing artificial added. To shop in the produce department of a grocery store with the goods under suspicion of having been poisoned was quite another thing.

But thanks to BearGenics, that was exactly the situation that the people of Oblivion found themselves in. They had grown used to it, fatalistically accepting the problem, to the point that many of them did not expend much time and energy thinking about it. Thus, they lived up to their name: the Oblivious.

It didn't help that BearGenics and Natural Manipulators had advertisements on television and radio, in newspapers and magazines, and on the Internet. The ads made the use of Potions glamorous, as if an action hero in a movie were killing unwanted plants – weeds – by wielding them. Children saw these ads and were seduced from an early age by pretty images and catchy tunes, all about Pestituted foods. Nature had no budget with which to promote itself.

What had BearGenics done to their food?

It had recruited people with Ph.D.s to work in its laboratories, people who were using their knowledge to do damage rather than undo it. These people held graduate degrees in biology, chemistry, biochemistry, genetics, botany, and entomology (the study of insects). These scientists spent their careers working to splice poisons into planet genes.

Genetics, the study of DNA – deoxyribonucleic acid – is the study of the basic code of life. Everything in Nature has a genetic code: plants, animals, humans, you name it. Raspberries, honey bees, wheat, corn, squash, apples…the list is as long as the list of discovered and undiscovered species on the entire planet Earth.

Genes pass on their codes through reproduction, which is accomplished differently depending upon the species involved, and internally, with something called messenger RNA (ribonucleic acid). Messenger RNA splits off and replicates within an organism to make it grow once produced. But to produce one of anything, DNA is necessary, and it is passed along via pollination in plants.

These travesties of scientists spent their careers tinkering with plant DNA, altering it to contain poisons so that, as each plant grew in the field, it had insecticides built right into it. They were known as Potionists both within and outside of their industry.

Each Potionist was paid enough money (and then some) to afford large houses, luxury vacations, expensive cars, and private educations for their children with no student loans to hobble them in their future working lives. Obviously, these were people who could be bribed.

The mascot for BearGenics was a black bear in a lab coat with round spectacles. His lab coat pocket had a logo that depicted a test tube with a plant growing out of it. The expression on the bear's face was not as benign; it was stern and serious, projecting an aura of stern rigidity and authority.

Natural Manipulators was full of ironies, yet it somehow failed to appreciate this. Its logo was the same one that was on the lab coat pocket of the BearGenics bear. Why?

Because BearGenics was the parent corporation of Natural Manipulators! Natural Manipulators supplied BearGenics with the poisons that its Potionists used, and it employed its own Potionists to prepare these potions. In fact, if one thought about the logo for BearGenics, one would see that the bear in the lab coat was just an anthropomorphized Potionist.

Natural Manipulators had production facilities all over the land of Oblivion. This saved some product distribution costs. One of its teams of Potionists worked to integrate their products into solid form. The systemic pesticides that it produced looked like small red pellets, which were stored in large burlap bags. The bags had the test-tube plant logo on one side, and red skull-and-crossbones on the other.

A huge, multi-billion dollar corporation, Natural Manipulators also supplied agribusinesses all over the land of Oblivion with a thing called Systemic Pesticide. The owners were its best customers, because they cared solely about production and maximum output. They did not understand or care how the natural world worked.

The Potionists, paid by the Pestitutes, published article after article in peer-reviewed scientific journals about their potions. These articles were deliberately slanted to present anything but the potions as the cause of damage to honey bees and the ecosystem. It was their fervent hope that anyone who read the articles would be seduced into forgetting who had written such illegitimate nonsense and that their agenda was to sell more potions.

The Potionists at BearGenics and Natural Manipulators thought that they were very clever and creative, but they were neither.

In fact, they were something known as stupid geniuses, which is what we call people who are incapable of comprehending the fact that just because one is capable of doing something, it doesn't mean that one should actually do it. Put another way, they were people with very high I.Q. (Intelligence Quotient) scores – numbers from standardized tests that measure…or attempt to measure…how smart a person is – but without wisdom.

The Thieves were simply fools who bought the use of that capability, a thing that had taken them no discipline to attain, and waited for a product to be created from it. After that, they put a label on it and sold it, caring not a whit for whatever damage it would do, nor about the fact that once released, the potion would be uncontrollable.

Once released, it would multiply exponentially in Nature.

Once Nature gets something, it does not need human help to grow or destroy anything. It is powerful, independent, and indifferent to human agendas.

That lesson is one that the Thieves never stopped to consider, let alone learn.

The Founding Mother

In addition to the Founders of its political system, Oblivion had a Founding Mother of its environmental movement, a woman who was an expert in chemistry, biology, botany, and entomology. She was a true scientist: ethical, not driven by profit but by respect for Nature.

She understood the damage that insecticides were doing to the natural world – to humans, to animals, to fish and other aquatic creatures, to plants, and to insects.

She knew – and more importantly, she pointed out – the fact that insecticides kill all insects indiscriminately, even the ones that humans don't want killed.

Several decades ago, she wrote a famous treatise about what insecticides were doing to the environment. She spent years gathering notes and data, researching what was happening to plants, animals, and insects on farms, in orchards, in forests, in residential neighborhoods, and in cities. Once her material was complete, she wrote her life's work and published it.

She was determined to tell the world – and the citizens of Oblivion – what the poisons do.

These poisons were being sprayed on wild plants to kill weeds, but they kill everything that they came into contact with. Then the weeds, which were the strongest of the plants to be sprayed, grew back bigger than ever, crowding out the ones that the sprayers had hoped to save.

Insecticides were sprayed over forests and lakes, and many insects did in fact disappear.

Those insects were the ones that had annoyed humans when they went fishing or hiking.

No thought was given to the consequences of doing away with the annoyance until the deed was done and the next season came to pass.

Then it was noticed that the insects that some beautiful ducks and eagles needed to eat were gone. Soon those beautiful ducks and eagles were also dwindling. Veterinarians and volunteers at animal sanctuaries tried desperately to save the few eagles that they found struggling in the wild. They fed and raised them, and years later released the hatchlings, hoping that they would be okay. Many weren't able to fend for themselves.

Salmon in the rivers that depended upon the insects above their waters soon had nothing to eat in areas that were sprayed. Their species nearly collapsed. The blueberries in the forests near those rivers barely grew. When the spraying was stopped, they recovered, but that was decades ago, before the intensity of the insecticides was increased.

Towns and counties all over Oblivion tried to kill weeds and annoying insects the same way, spraying overhead without warning residents. Cats that were outside at the time got poisons on their fur and paws, licked themselves clean, suffered terribly, and died. Many humans who happened to be out in their yards got terribly sick, suffering terribly with burning sensations in their eyes and on their skin. Months later, they were found to have illnesses that had mutated their DNA, and they were dying.

Fruit crops were sprayed, with similar effects.

The list went on and on.

The toxins sprayed on croplands killed the soil.

Normal soil is full of microbes and biomes that facilitate crop growth. There are earthworms that live on these things. Dead soil lacks the necessary nutrients for crop growth. The Founding Mother did her best to warn that this would happen if the insecticide use was allowed to continue, to no avail.

The Founding Mother was called to the Marble City to defend her treatise to politicians whose campaigns had been financed by the Thieves, but her work was impeccable and irrefutable. Her work withstood every attack because her research had been so careful and relentless. It was just too thorough to impeach, so they gave up.

The treatise that the Founding Mother had written became a classic, one of those books that is praised but seldom read. That definition of a classic was provided century earlier by a famous author who was very funny, always right about what he said, and yet popular.

It is, unfortunately, a very rare thing to be both popular and right.

A scientist who is right cannot hope to be popular without painful lessons that have already been learned. But what scientist is talking about lessons already learned?

A warning is not enough to produce an emotional response.

And it is only when people get emotional about something that they take action.

That is the disability that scientists labor under.

If only a scientist had the advantage of being either entertaining or terrifying.

The Founding Mother did her best, but her treatise was lengthy and detailed.

Hopefully, this story will do what she tried to do.

If you want to know the full, horrific details after reading this preview, it is there.

This story is but a movie trailer to an epic tale.

Nature is Not the Enemy

The Thieves who owned and ran BearGenics and Natural Manipulators believed that Nature was not the friend of human beings.

More precisely, they believed that Nature was not the friend of big agribusinesses.

The simple fact of life – and of Nature – was that no crop could be expected to yield one hundred percent of its production undamaged and entirely for the use of humans.

…and why should it?

Nature needed some of what grew, specifically for insects, small animals, and birds.

BearGenics and Natural Manipulators did not care about that. It wanted it ALL to sell.

After all, humans paid it and its primary customers – agribusinesses – for what grew.

Birds, animals, and insects generated no invoices, no payments, and no profits. They simply took a third of everything, which was Nature's way of exacting payment for what it made possible: food.

But that was of no consequence to Natural Manipulators or BearGenics.

The Thieves wanted it all.

Accordingly, they waged war on Nature.

They pushed Nature to produce more and more and more, constantly and without rest.

The Founding Mother's treatise with its main lesson, which was that Nature is not the enemy, was ignored.

Nature, an all-powerful, indifferent, and unstoppable force, was arrogantly ignored.

Nature was treated instead as a resource to be harnessed, one that has no limits.

It is not.

Queening and Re-Queening

Queening is a natural part of a beehive's life cycle, which, under natural conditions, is never-ending. Every few years, the queen bee reaches the end of her reproducing life and is killed by her handlers. She is then superseded by one of the newborn – fresh out of their cell from being grown as pupae by the nurse bees with extra royal jelly – queen bees.

Which one?

Why, whichever of them manages to win a fight to the death among the others.

Supersedure is a nasty business, but it is part of Nature.

The benefit of this is that the hive carries on its genetic material via one of these queens.

She is strong, she has been raised on the immune-boosting food of the hive, and she will live for 2 or 3 years after her virgin flight, during which she mates with as many drones as possible. Thus, she will have millions of sperm stored up from this one and only flight, and lay more than her weight in eggs every day.

At least, that's how it works if Nature is in charge.

Queen, with green dot, walking around on a frame among worker bees – all female.

Some few beekeepers in Oblivion wisely left Nature in charge.

The rest, those who were involved with big agribusinesses, did not.

They would find the queen of each of their hives, pinch her to death between their fingers, and re-queen each hive with mail-ordered queen bees. These unfortunate queens – the ones that had been mailed, had arrived either via the Oblivious Postal Service or by airplane…or both. They were stressed out from the journey, and hungry after being without the brood to feed and clean them for a few days.

The beekeepers had to be careful with their new charges as they re-queened each hive. Each one had to be put into the hive to exchange pheromones with her new family, but be sealed off, physically inaccessible to them while that was happening. If not, the new family would reject her – by killing her. The new queen would be sealed off with a candy plug, which the worker bees would eat off, by which time they would accept her.

Why do this at all?

They didn't want to wait the few weeks that the natural process of re-queening took! They were convinced that if they paused in their relentless work schedule, they would lose money, so they forced things along, hurrying a natural, normal phenomenon. With other stress-inducers in the mix, they soon found themselves doing this every year, because their queens grew weaker and weaker along with their entire hives.

As if that weren't bad enough, a company called BeeGenics had been artificially substituting the natural process of the virgin flight of a queen bee for a test tube, a syringe needle, and a pipette in its laboratories. Entomologists who thought they were very clever – but were actually rather foolish – called Supersedurists here – squeezed drones to death to get their genetic material out, then forced it into queen bees with pipettes. These were the queen bees that were being sent long-distance to new homes.

Some beekeepers only re-queened to strengthen their hives and to introduce biodiversity. Many of these individuals wisely did not make a habit of killing queen bees. They only did this to help the hives along and maintain what they had.

They did not buy queen bees from BeeGenics.

They bought them from Naturalists – beekeepers who lived quietly, communing with their bees in the countryside. The Naturalist beekeepers grew queens slowly, and followed natural methods as closely as possible. They found queen larvae and isolated them from one another, keeping nurse bees clustered around each one to raise them.

It should come as no surprise that the Naturalists' hives were a lot healthier.

But they were a small minority in Oblivion, and their work did not make them wealthy.

The Oblivious beekeepers – the ones in a hurry to work nonstop and make their bees do the same – continued on their race of a routine as before. They had convinced themselves that they could not afford to change their behavior or wait for Nature.

They did not realize that if they failed to do exactly that, Nature would cease to cooperate.

Stress and Constant Travel

Honey bees need freedom from commutes and stress.

They need to spend their lives working with consistent routines and plenty of rest.

Humans, like bees, do better when we don't have to commute to a job in a city every day, or worse yet, take a long flight late at night to an early meeting in a faraway city.

Imagine you have a job with a big corporate entity that involves a daily commute to your office. You are a low- to mid-level employee, not highly paid. You have debts to pay, so you need this job. You won't be quitting and moving on to something else without reliable alternative, and such things are not easy to find.

Suddenly, your boss tells you to go home and pack; you're taking a late-night flight across the country to attend an early morning meeting. And here – study these talking points on the flight, which you must rush to catch.

Do you really think you will get enough food or sleep between now and then?

Do you really think you will arrive ready to negotiate any deal with the well-rested, well-fed team of representatives you will face the next morning at this other corporation's headquarters?

Do you think you will have time to buy and eat a healthy meal?

If you think so, you must be an optimist, a fool, or both.

You will be overtired, you will have eaten a salty snack on the plane with a sugary drink, and if you have any chance for a real meal, it will likely be a cheap one from a fast-food joint, also high in salt and sugar, plus fat and mystery ingredients.

[That is another story, but the idea is the same as what BearGenics and Natural Manipulators do. The only difference is that the target consumers are restaurants, grocery stores, and the people who shop in them.]

Now suppose that your boss springs these excursions on you without notice often.

What effect would that have on your health and sanity?

It can't be a good one.

You will come into contact with many people, places, and situations.

As you do all of this, you – overtired and not eating properly – will have less strength with which to resist every cold, virus, bacteria, and who knows what other toxin you encounter.

You will get sick after a while.

This is what Thieving humans were doing to the bees.

Big agribusinesses hired beekeepers to come and pollinate their crops all over Oblivion.

The bees wintered in the south, which was home for many of them, feasting on the pollen and nectar of orange blossoms and wild tupelo peppers. That ought to have been enough activity for them, but no – there was no rest for the honey bees. The Thieves insisted that they must be somewhere that produced pollen all year, because that would lead to more crop production.

Most honey bees were not lucky enough to have the observant beekeeper that I described previously, who watched her bees and didn't demand too much honey from them. No...instead of taking only what the bees could spare, most beekeepers relied on their hives for their entire income. They needed rental fees from farmers and agribusinesses for the services of their unwitting apiaries. They had grown used to being able to constantly harvest honey.

Most citizens were as Oblivious to the damage as their nation's name implied.

The beekeepers who participated in this practice knew it was dangerous to the bees' health, but they didn't stop because this had worked for so long that they just kept it up until they couldn't.

So the bees spent their springs in the west, pollinating almond orchards, and their summers in the mid-northwest in the clover fields. Others went straight from the almond orchards to the blueberry patches in the southeast, then headed up the coast, northeast, to apple and cherry orchards, all the way to the northeastern tip of Oblivion for more blueberries, then back in the opposite direction for pumpkin patches. Pumpkins are a variety of squash, and squash plants have flowers. No rest for the weary!

Instead of an overnight airplane ride, the bees were treated to an overnight truck ride.

Their hives were stacked on tractor-trailer trucks, which used the carbon dioxide-infused highways of Oblivion to get from place to another. The constant noise of the highway was not something that they could hear, but the vibrations of those sounds caused them nonstop stress.

This was not good for the bees. They arrived for each job exhausted and stressed, a bit confused by new surroundings, and then had their hives situated in some random orchard or field. Some were dead, including a few queen bees, and the stage was set for collapse.

The beekeepers snapped on cages with replacement queen bees, waited a day or so, then let the queens out. Where had these queens come from? A variety of places, both in and out of Oblivion. Some were from science labs, and had been provided with genetic material from far fewer drones than they would have found on their own, in Nature.

They would be fed junk food: high-fructose corn syrup treated with antibiotics. This stuff permanently altered the honey that the bees produced. It also altered the bees, weakening them with each generation that consumed it. Any human who ate that honey would be resistant to those antibiotics if they got sick.

Finally, their beekeeper, the human whose presence they are used to, left them. Then what?

Out went the hives' scouts to scope out the area and see what there was to collect. As they moved about, they came into contact with other weary travelers from other apiaries around the huge nation of Oblivion. Whatever pathogens those bees had – whatever cold, whatever illness – the odds were high that they would catch the same ailments.

The Potionists developed artificially sweetened liquids to put into beehives, because big agribusinesses wanted mass-produced crops and honey. The purpose of this was to feed bees when they weren't making lots of honey naturally, just to keep the hives fully awake, energized, and ready to go out and pollinate crops year-round.

The owners of the orchards who had paid a rental fee may have realized that the bees they had hired were not functioning at optimal levels and complained, but what did they expect? This was apian slavery, and the slaves were overworked. Complain all you want, but scientific facts are objective, and cannot be changed by emotion or legal action. The bees would stay sick unless and until they were able to rest and recover.

Big agribusiness was killing them with stress and exposure to toxins and communicable viruses. This was just one thing of many that was happening to the honey bees.

Not all of it was done by humans. Some of it was done by Nature, and some of what Nature did could be mitigated or even prevented if humans observed bees rather than used them as a resource.

But…only a few humans did that.

Anyone who demands too much of honey bees – which is the same as demanding it of Nature itself – gets what they deserve.

Humans had not equated the needs of the bees with their own. When you introduce such blatant selfishness to the mix, this is the result: bees on the brink of collapse.

Systemic Insecticides

The Potionists at Natural Manipulators had created so many insecticides that farmers, orchard growers, and agribusinesses had quite a menu of them to choose from. They used several different kinds each growing season, only stopping a few weeks before it was time to harvest their crops, assuming that this would keep the poisons from making the food dangerous to eat.

They were wrong.

The honey bees went out to pollinate the almonds, the berries, the peaches, the apples, and various other crops shortly after and often during insecticide use. The schedules were not monitored closely enough by farmers, who were only renting the hives from apiaries. The farmers lacked the vested interest that beekeepers had in the hives, and beekeepers lacked the clout to insist that farmers hold back on insecticide use.

As if that weren't enough to contend with, people used insecticides on their flower gardens and lawns. They were determined to have a monocrop of flawless, uninterrupted green grass. This made it impossible for hobbyist beekeepers in neighborhoods of homes – houses, condominiums, and apartments – to keep their bees alive and healthy. When the bees went out to forage, few escaped the effects of the insecticides.

Legal protection was only partially provided for wildlife refuges, and bees foraged there also.

Added to that problem was the damage done – bred into – the plants by BearGenics. The Potions were a part of the genetic structure of the plants, after all. Bees are attracted to sunflowers, canola flowers, corn tassels, and many other plants, all of which had been tampered with by BearGenics. Either way – whether pollinating plants that were or were not sprayed – the honey bees came into contact with the Potions. What was in these Potions that hurt the bees?

Neurotoxins! Neurotoxins are poisons that attack the nervous system. They affect memory, the ability to learn, and navigation. This was why bees got lost and never made it home to their hives – why they died alone, in some unknown spot, not to be found. These Potions had chemical names such as neonicotinoids and neonics, which had molecular structures in common with tobacco plants.

The people of Oblivion knew that nicotine was a dangerous poison because the Observers had run a news show that had told them so. In it, a Potionist had become a Whistleblower – telling the world what evil deeds went on in secret – because he could no longer bear to assist the Thieves. Undeterred and addicted, they puffed away, happy to forget, Oblivious.

They failed to notice that nicotine was a part of the plants they ate. They ignored the fact that their food supply was tainted from start to finish until the problem was systemic, both in the plants and in the food production process. They overlooked the fact that anyone using a potion had to wear a special protective suit just to avoid touching or inhaling any of what was sprayed. They did not pay attention to the fact that bees were dying around them.

Lost in Transit

Once the toxins were inside the honey bees, the effect they had on them was permanent.

The honey bees were high on toxins, flying around with permanent nerve and brain damage, getting lost. Unable to get home in the twenty-four hours that Nature required of them before they ran out of energy, most of them stayed lost and died. As for the few who did make it back to their hives, they brought the toxins with them, poisoning the food supply that the younger bees and the queen lived on.

As if that wasn't enough, honey bees were not the only species to suffer.

There were many other species of bees all over the planet, each indigenous to a particular area, each with differing sizes, shapes, and yet the same black-and-yellow furry stripes, and the same fuzzy disposition. They were all content to gather pollen and drink nectar, and all liked sweet-smelling, beautiful flowers.

But they were all coming into contact with neurotoxins – neonicotinoids – and dying, lost.

This was the land of Oblivion, so no one noticed until the damage was done.

Nosema – Gut Mold

Okay, it's not called gut mold; that definition was added to grab your attention with disgust.

No doubt it worked…

Nosema is the scientific term for a microspore that forms on bees' intestines. It usually invades beehives as winter sets in, leaving them sick and too weak to forage when spring comes.

So what? What role could human behavior play in nosema?

A significant one, of course, thanks to the Potionists.

They had developed a menu of nasty mixtures that targeted mold, called fungicides.

Entomologists, frustrated to hear of the difficulties that beekeepers had with nosema, studied the effects of fungicides.

Yes, they did preserve fruits and other produce from destruction by molds.

But…honey bees that came into contact with fungicides had a lowered resistance to nosema.

How could this be? Nosema is a kind of mold, isn't it?

Well, yes, but like insecticides, any life form that is repeatedly attacked by a poison develops a resistance to it after a while, and this is true of fungicides also.

When honey bees flew over plants that had been dosed with fungicides – or worse, were being dosed as the bees flew over them and pollinated them – they were exposed to those Potions.

This counterintuitive outcome may be due to two contributing mechanisms. One is that strains of nosema that survive fungicide exposure may have a particularly virulent capacity to damage bee physiology. A second explanation may have to do with the effect of fungicides on the normal innate resistance bees have to fungal infestations. Thus compromised, the bees were unable to fight off mold infestations.

Undeterred, the Potionists at Natural Manipulators continued to make more fungicides, and the Pressure-Pointers continued to push for their use, arguing that they were necessary for the preservation of the crops. Without a way to keep mold from forming on fruits, they insisted, the entire effort of food production would fail.

The Naturalists pointed out that without healthy honey bees, the entire effort was pointless, but their voices were drowned out yet again by those of the Thieves and their attorneys.

Mites and Other Parasites

Mites plague beehives, honey bees, and beekeepers all year.

They come in several varieties of nuisance.

The most common one is the varroa, which feast on bodily fluids of bee pupae, infecting their bloodstreams with parasitic material that weakens their immune systems, causing those bees to have deformed wings, and acarine, which lay eggs in bee tracheas. As you might expect, breathing with intruder eggs in one's trachea is problematic.

Varroa mite on bee larvae.

Another common invader of beehives is the small hive beetle, the larvae of which tunnel into a hive, right through its honeycomb and into the honey supply, which they eat and defecate in, ruining it. The honey then stinks of rotten oranges.

Still another is the wax moth. The wax moth feeds on beeswax, which the bees use to build honeycomb, house larvae, and hold honey in place. Without it, the honey oozes out, ruined and wasted.

The list of naturally-occurring attackers of honey bees goes on and on: bacteria called foulbrood, fungal diseases with names such as chalkbrood and stonebrood, and viral ones that cause paralysis, discoloration, and wing failure.

All of these things, combined with the pressures put on them by human use of honey bee services and other human activities in the ecosystem, added more pressure on the bees' ability to cope and survive.

But fear not! Beekeepers were not forgotten by Natural Manipulators, whose Potionists had prepared a mixture to deploy against the mites: Thymalisman. It contained a chemical found in thyme, a natural herb, but that was where the natural aspect of the potion ended. From there on, it was a toxin. Humans were warned to wear gloves when handling this product, which came in gel form, wrapped in foil or sealed in buckets, or on pads that could be stuck in hives.

Too much direct contact – wow…how much is too much?! – would lead to skin, lung, and scrotal cancer and, not surprisingly, death. Don't inhale. Why was this so dangerous?

Just look at the ratio of the Thymalisman content in a one-pound bunch of thyme to 25 grams of the Potion: it was the same, but super-concentrated. Anything found in Nature can be a nutrient if ingested in small amounts, but a poison in large amounts.

The Potionists knew this. That is not an issue to them, however. Their agenda was to formulate a Potion that beekeepers could be persuaded to use against mites. Because there weren't many options in existence, beekeepers would give anything a try. The bees didn't like this thyme-based Potion, either. Why should they if it was such a threat to their human beekeepers?!

It stank, and they would fan madly to get the stench out. Next, the bees propolized it over (used propolis – the tree sap mentioned previously), effectively sealing it off, cloaking the stench until it is stamped out, and the rejection was a fait accompli. If the beekeeper used Thymalisman too aggressively, and for longer than 3 weeks and 3 days, or all in one treatment, it could poison the bees, thus defeating its own purpose.

The Potion also had the unfortunate effect of flavoring, er, tainting the honey.

There had to be a better way to help the bees survive.

Eventually, beekeepers would balk at doing the same thing year after year as the effectiveness of a Potion waned. At that point, they would look for other solutions.

The Founding Mother had had some great insights to offer, but almost no one cared to listen to her advice. Perhaps, before the environment was completely stripped of its ability to benefit from it, the Naturalists suggested, the people of Oblivion might want to consider it.

The Founding Mother had suggested enlisting entomologists who were not Potionists to deploy insects that were the natural enemies of any problem insect against that problem insect.

But...Natural Manipulators wouldn't benefit financially from that approach! But – so what?! It was time for the lawmakers to stop caring about that before it was too late.

Meanwhile, some of the beekeepers tried changing the design of the hives that they built to more closely resemble the ones that bees built in Nature. These beekeepers were usually the ones who were willing to live close to Nature, in near poverty, and alone, as beekeepers used to do before the Thieves managed to turn almost everything into an "industry".

The beehives that they constructed did not use the same wax frames as before.

There were 2 changes. One was in the shape of the frames. Remember those that I described earlier, which were tapered at the bottom? Some beekeepers tried these. The other was in the sizes of the hexagonal cells in the wax itself.

A top-frame hive.

Instead of a uniform size that was a bit larger than the bees seemed to prefer, and which left enough room for mites to settle in, these wax cells were of graduated sizes. The cells were smaller at the tapered bottom of each frame, then a bit larger, and finally the old size at the top.

Inside the top-frame hive: bees make a variety of hexagonal cell sizes.

This aided the bees considerably. They were able to save more pupae because there was no room for mites to sneak in, whereas before the nurse bees had been uncapping them to oust the invaders, along with the pupae. Farther out from the deep interior of the hive, the bees could afford to pick and fuss over a larger cell, but not all of them – only near the exterior.

One frame pulled from a top-frame hive, with bee-made hexagonal cells of varying sizes.

These beekeepers also stopped using mite-killing chemicals, preferring to let the bees evolve to resist mites rather than having mites get stronger and stronger as they evolved to resist Potions. Those who adopted such methods sat and watched and waited, separated from the Thieves and the mass-production method of the food industry.

These beekeepers bravely did without many of life's luxuries. Instead of seeking money, they looked for other kinds of wealth in the environment around them.

But there were very few of them, and very many who were determined to work with the Thieves as they had before. They accepted the Potions, hoping that if they followed the manufacturer's instructions, the honey they harvested would not taste funny and not have mite feces in it, and that they would not poison themselves in the process of using the Potions.

There is hope, and then there is reality. One cannot live in both.

Drought

Bees need moisture to make honey.

This simple fact must not be forgotten, especially during a drought.

It's what they use for the reductions of nectar, combined with their own enzymes, to make honey. A bee will spend much of a day on this, sloshing the nectar around in its mouth until it becomes not the sweet sugar was extracted from a flower but a syrupy fructose.

What starts off as a mixture of 70 percent water and 30 percent remaining components is reduced first to a ratio of 40 percent water to 60 remaining components. Next, the bee proceeds with the final phase of conversion, fanning what it has created thus far with its wings. This continues until the ratio of water to other is 20 to 80. At that point, it's honey.

It doesn't take much to realize that without sufficient water, this won't be happening.

So what's the problem about getting bees enough water to work with?

Didn't it rain?

Didn't that fill up every living thing with enough moisture?

What about rivers, streams, ponds, lakes, and aquifers?

Bad news: human population had grown so much in Oblivion, and human food choices had become so diversified, that the demands placed upon the water supply exceeded it.

More bad news: this stress was not just in Oblivion – it was all over the planet.

Still more bad news: human overpopulation had led to more people using more fuel to heat their homes, cool their homes, and run machines such as cars, factories, and the Internet. This had heated up the atmosphere, and led to flash floods in some geographic areas – which could wash away everything, not only insect life – and too little rainfall in other areas.

There you have it: drought.

Drought can be caused by insufficient rainfall, a lowering water table underground, or a combination of both. With no relief in sight as humans relentlessly demand more and more from Nature, Nature wouldn't accede to enough of those demands to feed them all. It couldn't.

This was too much for Nature, and too much for the bees. The bees would not find enough healthy plants to pollinate or draw nectar from under such conditions.

Colony Collapse Disorder

In Nature, everything is connected...unfortunately.

Mess with one thing, you mess with it all.

Ruin one aspect of a delicate, intricate system, and the destruction spreads.

It's like a set of dominoes, falling in whatever pattern they started in.

Constellations of collapse...

The problem had the somewhat vague name of colony collapse disorder.

Honey bee colonies collapsed under the relentless and combined pressures put on them by:

1. Stress and constant travel;

2. Neurotoxins in the neonicotinoids and neonics that they encountered in the plants they touched, drank from, and gathered pollen from;

3. Fungicides that crashed their natural ability to fight off mold infestations;

4. Mites and the poisons that the beekeepers attempted to repel them with;

5. Drought; and

6. Other, unidentified problems.

Scientists did not agree that any one stressor was the cause of it.

Naturalists, both lawyers and scientists among them, suggested that the pressure be removed from the honey bees. Stop requiring that they work to exhaustion. Don't make them travel to faraway crops, orchards, fields, whatever. Let them stay home and produce whatever amount of honey they can without requiring that they work to support the food production system.

What?! Let them rest?

What about the almond crop?! Oblivion produced over 80 percent of the world's crop!

Let it go? Why?!

To save the bees, of course, said the Naturalists. It would be far better to have some bees that still produced honey than none at all. It would also be far better to change the way that Oblivion produced crops than to go on the same way, because that way was leading to other kinds of collapse than just that of the honey bees. The whole system could collapse!

The focus ought to shift to maintaining resilience – crop resilience, hive resilience, systemic resilience. Stop using Potions and let Nature take over, and take whatever amount of food it offers without demanding more.

No more spraying, no more genetic splicing of plants. Just let them grow naturally, and plant untouched seeds, seeds that had not been worked over by BearGenics. Also, grow multiple crops rather than monocrops, because that was starving bees.

What a concept: instead of demanding constant growth and sustained, efficient production, require that each system maintain resilience.

This would prevent collapse.

Scaling back on human demands on Nature would also prevent exponential accrual of economic wealth. That is the cost of preventing collapse. The problem was that those who ran Oblivion – the Pestituters – would not accept that. They wanted constant wealth and the luxury that it brought.

No sale with the Thieves, who controlled the system.

No…they wanted more and more and more forever, regardless of the limits to growth that Nature has. They didn't care about the reality of the situation. They were going to push and push for more, living only in the present while never thinking of the long-term effects.

It wasn't really a conscious plan, but it was the one they were going with.

Beekeepers looked frantically and helplessly into their hives at what they saw:

Very few bees, all of which were moving about aimlessly, not working with their usual, normal purposefulness on the tasks that the beekeepers expected them to be occupied with. They seemed lethargic and confused.

Even fewer bees.

Dead bees.

Empty hives.

It got worse and worse as time went on, and it was terrifying.

This terror went beyond the mere fear of a loss of one's livelihood.

What the beekeepers were seeing made them fear that Nature was out of balance.

They were right.

If this was happening to the honey bees, they wondered, what about other bees?

What would humans do without bees?

Humans would die, they knew, but now they were thinking it consciously rather than merely in the back of their minds. The idea haunted them.

Beekeepers' Empty Hives

The Potionists had created monsters that entered the natural world and permanently altered the environment for the worse. Once introduced, the potions could not be removed. Nature took over, blowing seeds every which way, mutating them under the stress of sprayed-on potions and in-bred ones.

Bees from the hives kept by beekeepers – honey bees – as well as bumblebees and other honey-making bee species that lived in the untouched forests near almond and apple orchards, orange groves, raspberry patches, and farmlands, came into contact with these insecticides and were poisoned on contact with them.

The bees were not returning to their hives.

Instead, they were dying somewhere out in the fields, unable to navigate back.

They had gone out to work and been fatally injured on the job.

They had counted upon Nature to be as it ought to be – free of toxins – and it wasn't.

Bees are very trusting creatures, as well they should be. They trust that any plant that they land on in their quest for nectar and pollen will not be toxic to them. If it attracts them, it must be safe. Because they only have 10 taste receptors, they can't detect toxins.

That is why the beekeepers and academic scientists were so angry: the Thieves were all pestituted to the Potionists and vice versa, they said. They discussed the details at beekeeping conferences, and in cyberspace in their blogs. They wrote about what was wrong in their scientific journal articles, and gave interviews to the Observers.

They made sure to point out that:

All of the seeds were pestituted – poisoned with insecticides that indiscriminately targeted all insects, not specific ones. This left the bees at the mercy of any plant that they landed on and tried to get nectar from, contaminating that product, just as the plants were contaminated.

All food that anyone – human or animal or insect – ingested was hence infested with poison.

It was genetically engineered into the chemical structure of each plant at the molecular level, cross-bred into each plant, and distributed as seeds to as many farms as possible.

Once this was done, the trouble multiplied exponentially into infinity.

There was no stopping it.

There was no stopping the inescapable spread of the seeds through the wind and into the fields of neighboring farms whose farmers wanted only natural plants growing on their land – organic, they called it.

Nature had combined forces – unwittingly, but inextricably – with genetically engineered ones. The seeds that blew over property lines mixed with those that the farmers had chosen to work with. Soon those farmers, who knew better than to mess with the natural genetic structure of the plants, were at the mercy of those who didn't.

The seeds took root in their fields, and the Thieves demanded a share of the profits from the crops grown by the organic farmers.

Never mind that the organic farmers had made no contracts with the Thieves.

Never mind that they did not buy any of their pestituted seeds.

No...never mind any of that, said the Thieves, because it does not matter.

It does not matter as a matter of law.

The farmers were amazed and puzzled.

How could they become trapped into a binding business relationship with an entity that they had not deliberately sought out?!

The Courts had an answer for that, one that was handed down when BearGenics' attorneys were finished arguing their case: the farmers had, however inadvertently, grown crops with the seeds of BearGenics, and since BearGenics owned all of its seeds in perpetuity, any products grown with those seeds belonged in part to that corporation.

This meant that any farmer, thanks to the power of wind, could find him or herself trapped in a business relationship with BearGenics, forced to grow abominated crops that he or she did not trust or want anything to do with.

Not only that, but the farmers were trapped in that situation in perpetuity, often unable to earn enough money to continue in business as farmers as BearGenics snatched more and more of their profits. More and more of them were forced to sell off their land to huge agribusinesses that worked with BearGenics.

The family farm, and natural, organic foods, were rapidly turned into things of the past.

The Fairy Tale Princess's Fruit

Ironically enough, people in Oblivion had all grown up reading a fairy tale in which a princess was fed poisoned fruit. This princess ought to have known better than to have eaten the fruit she was offered, but she ate it anyway and suffered alarming consequences.

Let's consider the fruit that she was offered.

It smelled sweet and enticing.

Its shape was uniform and round, and it sat neatly in her hand when she held it.

It had lovely, vibrant colors, fading from bright to pale with a smooth transition.

It had no flaws that she could see or taste, neither before nor after she bit into it – because not one insect had touched it.

Why not?

Well, those who grew up in Oblivion knew the reason: the evil one who offered it to her had dipped it in a poison potion that she had formulated in her laboratory.

Why had the princess been willing to listen to this evil one?

Well, she did smile sweetly, and represent her product to be perfect, desirable, and harmless.

Rather than checking with anyone else about either the fruit or its source, the princess had eagerly reached for the fruit and enjoyed a bite of it. She had found it easier and simpler to just believe the smiling fruit bringer than to question either the product or the evil one.

Why didn't she question anything?

Well, the evil one didn't seem evil to the princess. The fruit was offered with a smile and an enticing description. What could possibly be wrong with it, she thought, and took it.

The princess gave no thought to the evil one's motives.

Now why do I say that this is ironic?

Well, it ought to sound very familiar.

The author of that ancient fairy tale had done his best to warn the reader not to trust blindly, to question what life presented, and to beware of strangers bearing unknown goods, but as the people of Oblivion grew up, they forgot this lesson and took the fruit and ate it.

They didn't have to.

The answers to all of these questions were not concealed.

First, there was the appearance of the fruits, which bore a startling similarity to what the fairy tale princess was offered – they were just too perfect to be natural.

To add insult to injury, the natural fruits cost more than the fairy-tale fruits. This induced most of the people of Oblivion to choose the cheaper ones, of course.

The fruits were also far larger than naturally-grown, organic ones.

Fairy-tale peach at left, natural, organic one at right.

Another difference was the almost complete lack of taste to the fairy tale princess's fruit. The organic fruit was much juicier and had a lot more flavor.

Next, there was the sales pitch offered by the agribusinesses, telling people how great their products were.

Finally, there were ways to question what was offered: stickers on fruits that told what corporation sold them and what geographic location they came from, labels on boxes that the fruits came in that listed the potions bred into and sprayed upon them. As if that wasn't enough data, a customer had the option of researching the origins of each product over the Internet.

What did those labels say was in and on the fruit?

It was disturbing, as it should be. The fruit was "treated with" three different potions, all aimed at killing mold, commonly called fungicides, and coated with wax.

Washing the fruit would not remove the wax, though some people did attempt to do so, using a scrub-brush over their kitchen sinks with warm water running over the fruits.

Not mentioned on the labels and boxes was the fact – which could be found online – that insecticides had been sprayed multiple times onto the fruits as they grew. More often than not, this was done while migrant workers who were paid a pittance to pick the fruit were either doing so or else close by. These workers suffered terrible skin rashes, eye damage, and lung injuries.

And of course the honey bees that had been trucked to the orchards where this was done had buzzed on through, pollinating the flowers on those fruit trees, thus making the fruit grow, then flying off with chemical poison, disoriented, unable to return to their hives. They never made it back to continue their hives' existence. They fell somewhere away from home, dizzy and exhausted, and died.

None of this was kept a secret; the Observers had diligently reported it all.

There was nothing that the Pestituters could do about that.

But...most people didn't bother to investigate any of this.

It was far easier to just buy and eat.

And why be careful when the government of Oblivion was checking everything?

The FDA – Fairy Dope Administration – was charged with making sure that the food that the public bought in grocery stores was safe for human consumption. Most of the people of Oblivion never bothered to research the FDA's record-keeping standards. If they had, they would have been alarmed, because those standards had been adopted by the FDA from the food production industry and not from academia.

Good Laboratory Practice (GLP) was the term that the Potionists used to describe their system, claiming that it prevented fraud. But the director of the Oblivious Institute of Health was not impressed. She pointed out that academic quality controls were of higher quality and had the added benefit of being unbiased by motivations such as financial gain. Under the relentless onslaught of the Thieves' Pressure-Pointers, the FDA continued to use the Potionists' standards.

It was a lot like the life of the fairy tale princess. The only standard that the evil one had to meet was her own, which matched that of other, similarly trained and similarly motivated evil ones. The only difference was the target – other evil ones were after other individual princesses.

Real life was not a fairy tale, however, so the events described in that story played out much more slowly, on the lives and health of all citizens in Oblivion, not just one.

Instead of instantly falling on the floor in a dead faint with no pulse or breath, people had to eat a lot more of these Pestituted fruits before there was any sign of trouble. This of course, suited the Thieves perfectly, enabling them to sell far more fruit.

The fruit's genetic structure carried micro-RNA, which are messenger genes. The Potionists had bred this into each one. It was part of the biochemical tampering that they were paid so much money to add to the fruits. The micro-RNA induced an early onset of the aging process. With this, came an increased susceptibility to cancer as tumor suppressor genes were interfered with – all delivered by those who offered such attractive, flawless-looking fruit with a seductive tone of voice and a smile in their advertisements.

This was the slow and insidious version of eating the fairy tale princess's fruit.

Death would come faster than it would if people were able to access natural fruit, however imperfect that fruit might appear. Natural fruit is safer, sweeter, and tastes much better.

Everything that is questioned and proven safe is worth the sacrifice required, but that takes more effort and vigilance.

Regardless of the time differential between the fairy tale and reality, the people of Oblivion continued to eat the fairy tale princess's fruit.

Differing Burdens and Standards

A long time ago, many of the people of Oblivion – those who founded it as a nation – moved there from the Land Across the Pond. I say many because there were already some people living on the land that came to be known as Oblivion. They were not the Oblivious – they were, and still are, the Native People.

Until recently, which means the last century, the Oblivious did not call it the Land Across the Pond. They only started doing so as a joke, because they were so proud of the technology they had created, technology that enabled them to go back there so quickly and efficiently.

Before that, it was an ocean to the Oblivious – a vast expanse that separated them from their former homes. Not anymore. Now they called that ocean a pond, because the world seemed so much smaller to them once they were able to traverse it so much faster, first via steamships and then by airplanes. Now it was the Land Across the Pond.

The people who lived in the Land Across the Pond had an older legal system, one that had different legal standards and different burdens of proof to meet.

The Land Across the Pond required anyone accused of rape or murder (just to give some extreme examples) to prove that they were innocent. The legal standard was guilty until proven innocent, with the burden on the accused. This situation worked in both criminal and civil cases, with life and liberty being at stake in criminal cases and money being at stake in civil ones.

To the Oblivious, for criminal court cases, that seemed grossly unfair – an inferior system.

The Founders reversed it, writing just the opposite into their laws.

With the legal standard that one was innocent until proven guilty, the accused had a much better chance of acquittal. This standard put the burden of proof onto the prosecutor, who worked for the government. Why create such a rule of law? To protect those who really are innocent from having their lives ruined by a mistake. If that meant that some criminals slipped away from the grasp of the law, and justice failed, so be it. The Founders were fed up with the opposite happening, as it had so often in the Land Across the Pond.

For a long time, this system was exactly what was needed and wanted in the Land of Oblivion, as fewer and fewer murderers and rapists slipped away as medical and scientific technology advanced. These advances enabled the prosecutors to prove cases and convict those who really were guilty, while also convincing them to drop cases against those who were not.

Wonderful! Everyone applauded and supported this.

But then the Pressure Pointers, the expensive attorneys who lacked a conscience and thought only of immediate financial benefit – both to themselves and to their clients – came along.

Their clients, who owned the large corporations – remember the Thieves? – wanted to use that legal standard and burden of proof for their own purposes. The Thieves wanted an easier time in court, an easier standard to meet – one that would not prevent them from selling anything and everything that their Potionists could create. They wanted a standard that would enable them to keep on selling their products, no matter how damaging those items were to the natural world that human beings depend on.

They ordered their attorneys to argue before the High Court that a corporation should have the same legal status as a person.

They did not think long-term, they did not think about consequences to future humans, and they did not care about anything but their own immediate profits and benefits.

The Thieves were not thinkers – they were users.

They typically came from families that did not include thinkers. These families could be wealthy or not, but the common denominator was a wish for more material comforts and for those comforts to be a permanent part of their lives. Comfort was like a drug to them.

It became a drug to their upper and mid-level employees as well. Like their bosses the Thieves, they each had a propensity for consuming resources to the point that they could not hold any more, then expelling them to make room for more. This is how they earned the name Corporate Puke. Both they and the Thieves were raised with excess, and they raised their children with it also.

They bought plastic toys for their children in garish colors, until there were 20 bicycles in a house with far fewer than 20 children. That seemed strange to the servants who worked for them, servants from other nations who were sending their wages home so that one child could have one bicycle. But, the servants needed the wages, so they just helped load the extra toys into their employers' vehicles without comment.

As teenagers, those same children were taught nothing about people elsewhere or about the pressure that they were putting on the planet's resources. New clothes, toys, electronic gadgets and whatever else struck their fancy were bought for them every week – or even every few days – and when the house was too full of junk, it was expelled from the home.

Where did it all go? Charities, thrift shops, and to the servants' rooms. This served as a metaphor for puking, hence one reason behind the moniker of Corporate Puke. The more that the mother in the family enjoyed shopping, the more was bought, and thus had to be ejected from the home periodically. This went on until children were in their late teens, and went away to college.

Away at school, they did as little studying as possible, just enough to pass and stay in school for the four years that it took to quality for an undergraduate degree…or maybe just little enough to stay for an extra year.

Why an extra year?

Well, Puking Parties were just too much fun!

Here, at the colleges and universities of Oblivion, puking was a staple of any corporate party.

The Puking Parties were held in Secret Society Houses. The students who lived in these houses felt a familial duty to earn places in them, because their fathers (the Secret Societies were all-male, dating back to the time of the Founders who, ironically, would have found them appalling) had had places in them when they were in college.

The students would wear bed sheets wound around themselves – always white ones – play music so loud that the campus police would eventually be called, and drink beer until they threw up. The smell after these parties was a horrendous combination: puke, urine, beer, and dog.

When their four or five years of pointless and mindless fun were up, the Secret Society boys went to work in the corporations, where they occasionally enjoyed a few more Puking Parties, and other excessive enjoyments. Hence, the full explanation behind the term Corporate Puke.

This had gone on for over a hundred years or more, since the Founding Forbears had died. It was after the Founders had died that their descendants had felt free to do what they wanted to do and party until they puked. No need to hold back without those eyes on them anymore…

The excesses got worse and worse – more and more extreme – until excess was taken for granted by the other students at Oblivion's colleges and universities, and by the administrators. The police would be called when the nuisance level rose to criminal behavior, but that was it.

These were the people running Oblivion's corporations, corporations that made insecticides.

And they wanted an easier legal standard to meet, one that would ensure their ability to sell the noxious chemicals that they were paying their scientists such high salaries to develop.

They set their Pressure-Pointing attorneys to the task, and were not disappointed.

The Pressure Pointers came up with the perfect solution: fight a case in court – civil court, not criminal – in which a corporation would then be declared to have the legal status and rights of a person.

The legal status and rights of a human being – a citizen of Oblivion – for a corporation!

They won it.

Now a corporation had only to assert that a product was safe, regardless of whether or not that was actually so, and leave it up to the government's attorneys to prove that.

But how?

Well…the judges in the Lower Courts and Justices of the High Court had once all been attorneys. That was normal – one learned how the legal system worked that way, after graduating from law school.

Some of those judges and Justices had worked for public interest groups, human rights groups, environmental groups, and other humanitarian and philanthropic organizations, called Naturalists.

Others had worked as Pressure Pointers for Corporate Pukes.

After all, Oblivion touted equal opportunity, equal rights, and equal time.

The problem with this system was that, gradually, as the Corporate Pukes raked in more money, they were able to pay for more, more, more of what they wanted, including Pressure Pointers.

Some of these attorneys went on to become judges and Justices, while others became politicians who had the legal authority to appoint them to these posts.

Sometimes a Naturalist attorney became a Justice, and sometimes it was a Pressure Pointer.

The Justices did not change their mindsets about what should and should not be the rule of law once they reached the High Court. No...their personal experiences and prejudices stayed with them, and affected their viewpoints and the Judgments that they wrote – Judgments that then became binding law.

This meant that as time went on, not only were the Naturalists fighting a steeply uphill legal battle against a legal standard, they were also fighting against a High Court with many Pressure Pointers for Justices.

The Naturalists – attorneys, judges, Justices, scientists, environmentalists, and citizens who concerned themselves with the natural world and how humans were affecting, changing, mutating, using, and abusing it – found themselves looking at the legal standard and burden of proof as a huge problem, and looking with longing at the system in the Land Across the Pond.

Yes, it was just the right thing for cases involving organic human beings.

But it was absolutely the wrong thing for cases involving soulless corporate entities.

These entities were not worthy of life, liberty, and a chance to pursue happiness like a living human being is.

They were merely words on paper, written into documents of incorporation and filed in some courthouse, usually in the State of Dementia. They were the products of humans who wanted money, not humans themselves.

Things had gone horridly wrong, spiraled out of control by greed and a lack of foresight.

Toxic Until Proven Innocent

The problem came down to having a legal standard and a burden of proof that protected the environment, and that placed that duty of protection above all else. Without that, the honey bees and all of the species that depended upon their efforts were doomed.

The Land Across the Pond, which was a small continent made up of many nations, had such a standard, one that was the reverse of Oblivion's. It said, prove that a toxin is safe before we will allow it to be used in Nature, and it placed the burden of doing so on BearGenics and Natural Manipulators. The Thieves couldn't meet that standard or prove that their products didn't cause irreparable harm, so they couldn't sell their poisons there.

Oblivion's Thieves were very frustrated and angry to find that, in the Land Across the Pond, their Potions were deemed toxic until proven innocent.

They would stay that way.

Oblivion needed a standard like that.

Corporations needed to be delisted as "persons" – declared to be the soulless entities they were, that existed to profit like locusts, at the expense of all other entities. As such, it should be much more difficult for them - not equal, and certainly not easier. After all, a corporation fretting about its profits was not a human being on trial for his or her life.

Being treated as a human being – a "person" – is a great legal principle for a murder trial of an individual, but it is moronic when applied to an environmental regulation. This before-the-fact leniency allows the damage to be done on a grand scale, enabling suicide by insecticide, and that made no sense.

But that is not so for a business. A business feels no pain or fear in court.

The only danger is to the profits of the Thieves, and since the Thieves were stealing, since they were arrogant users with no respect for others, granting their potential to profit from that any extra respect or additional protections was pure insanity.

Once the damage was done, there would be no going back.

No honey bees would mean no flowers. Humans loved to look at and smell flowers, and we enjoy perfumes and sachets made with them.

Oh, but that's just a luxury, you might say.

Luxuries are what make life worth living, I say back.

But that wasn't all that there was to not having healthy honey bees.

What about the fruits and vegetables?

Many humans were vegetarians, and the vegetarians were the healthiest of humans.

Not only that, but plants were what cows, chickens, and sheep ate.

How could farmers expect to raise those creatures without grass, alfalfa, and clover?

The answer is that they wouldn't be able to do so.

Well, that would take care of our food supply – gone!

There was fish, but the rivers, streams, ponds, and oceans were full of pesticides and other human-shed toxins, so Oblivion couldn't count on having enough of that, either.

It couldn't just form its diets from one category of foods and expect to be healthy.

Finally, no honey bees would mean no honey.

Locally produced honey helps with allergies and boosts the human immune system.

Oblivion was making a choice – a fatal one – to ignore what was happening to the bees.

Life is full of choices.

Oblivion had to see that humans must either make choices that protected everyone, or suffer.

The fate of the honey bees was just one case in point.

The Wisdom of the Land of the Fleur-de-Lis

While we are on the subject of laws in other nations versus laws in Oblivion, it seems worthwhile to describe one of those other nations, just to show the benefits of logic and proper appreciation for honey bees.

One of the nations across the pond from Oblivion was called Fleur-de-Lis. It was named, pointedly enough for this discussion, for a gorgeous flower that honey bees are attracted to and pollinate: the iris. The iris was the emblem of royalty there. The people of Fleur-de-Lis had disposed of their royalty, but not of their sense of beauty and of their reverence for that which gave them beautiful things: Nature.

It showed in everything that they made: the clothing, the architecture, the civil engineering projects, the interior décor, the artwork, and most of all, their food. Every dish was a work of art. The best chefs on the planet were trained in the Land of the Fleur-de-Lis. The food was delectable, all natural, grown by fussy, individual farmers and prepared by chefs who got irate if anyone so much as suggested that they make the slightest change to their ancient methods.

They were right to be that way.

The land of the Fleur-de-Lis was just one of those several nations on the Land Across the Pond, all of which were wiser than Oblivion when it came to the honey bees. When they had all banned the Potions and seeds of BearGenics and Natural Manipulators, much to the outrage of the Thieves who ran those corporate entities, the people of Fleur-de-Lis had been the most adamant about it.

It should be noted at this point that the honey bees evolved on the Land Across the Pond.

They were appreciated so much – the honey they produced was enjoyed so much – that when people moved from there to Oblivion, they brought honey bees with them. That way, they could continue to enjoy fruits and honey as before.

The people of Fleur-de-Lis insisted upon protecting the honey bees so that their raspberries, strawberries, flour, butter, and other ingredients would remain as pure as ever. Some of the people from Oblivion had been lucky enough to travel there and taste that food. The fruit tarts, they said, were the most perfect, wonderful, delectable, amazing things that they had ever tasted.

Good! Who wouldn't need and want more of that?!

However, in order to have any of that, there must be laws in place to protect it.

Laws must be watched carefully.

The trouble with laws – science and environmental laws, in this case – is that they don't simply last forever in a pristine, untouched form and thus solve a problem permanently. It is not realistic to make what seems like an ideal law and then sit back, satisfied that one's work is done and the problem won't resurface.

If left to sit on the books, a law gets stale. Loopholes – ways of avoiding compliance – are either found or created by clever, selfish individuals seeking temporary gain.

If a law is about protecting Nature, it must be strengthened from time to time, and checked on as often, to keep up with new discoveries and technologies.

If not, these things may either chip away at the effectiveness of a law or strengthen it. One can't be sure which of these outcomes will be the one, so the laws must be watched.

Laws must be changed periodically, just like diapers, and for the same reason.

Ironically, it was an Oblivious comedian who coined that phrase, referring to politicians.

Comedians provide social and political commentary and make a lot of sense.

Scientists, politicians, Observers, and citizens should listen to them.

Scientists can either help or hinder the legal process.

Their motives and biases depend upon their funding sources, which can be corporate, government, or academic. Of course, they do have a choice as to which one to work for, and they may also strike out on their own, taking a risk that they will or will not make money or achieve other goals.

Oblivion's politicians had a choice to make. They could either worry about their own careers, and pestitute themselves to stay in office after election, pandering to the Thieves, or they could focus their attention on what science told them. They could either kill the futures of Oblivion's descendants, or take a brave leap to protect them.

Observers must never stop pointing this out to the citizens everywhere in Oblivion.

This needed to be done for children at an early age, because children grew up to be voters, and politicians, and scientists, and observers. The Thieves were just a few of the nation, and they had to be outvoted and pushed back, or they would cause the deaths of everyone.

You might say that the Thieves must be included in that tally of "everyone" – but that still left the Oblivious dead of malnutrition, starvation, and misery…an unacceptable outcome.

That is why I am telling this story – to warn others not to elect politicians who allow this.

Without change, the Oblivious could not expect to survive and thrive. They certainly wouldn't end up like the people of Fleur-de-Lis, smelling of roses and irises. Instead, Oblivion would simply end up as a vile, stinking diaper, unfit for human habitation.

Preemptive Pressure Pointing

As if the lack of wisdom and foresight weren't enough of an obstacle in Oblivion, there was yet another legal barrier to contend with, and it too had been erected by Pressure Pointers.

It was called Preemption.

Here is how it worked: Oblivion was comprised of many geographic areas, called Districts, each of which had the right to make any law for itself that was not reserved by the national government. In addition, each District had the right to make national laws tougher – but not more lenient – within its boundaries. It followed that towns within those Districts would expect to do the same thing, and thus prevent insecticides from being sprayed on crop fields, yards, and other areas within their limits.

If lawn grooming corporations, which relied on insecticide use to make lawns uniformly green, could not legally pestitute themselves, perhaps the bees and the plants could survive untainted and thrive.

That sounded like a great principle to the people who wished to enact tougher rules locally.

Unfortunately, the corporations, as usual, could afford the most expensive and ruthless Pressure Pointers to approach the politicians who made laws in each District. They demanded that laws be passed that preempted local-level, town-made regulations, reserving the power to regulate insecticide use at the district level.

The district politicians agreed to do this, because they had no terms limits and so hoped to remain in office for their entire adult lives and careers, and because their campaigns were funded mostly by corporations. You guessed it: they were made to feel that they owed something to the corporations that made insecticides, such as BearGenics and Natural Manipulators.

The politicians at the district level were as Pestituted as the ones at the national level.

Pestitution took a lot of time and money, so the Pressure Pointers achieved different degrees of control in each District. Some Districts legislated Explicit Preemption, thus removing any control over any insecticide use from the towns. Others legislated that all authority to regulate insecticide use rested with a Board of Pestituters. Still other allowed towns to petition against the use of any insecticides within town limits. Finally, some few Districts did allow towns to control insecticide use within their geographic limits.

Districts' rights had brought about this variety, but the result was that out of 50, only 6 had managed to remain free of Preemption Laws.

"Oh, but the District can be counted upon to look after the towns' interests," the politicians had promised. That was as ridiculous as saying that giving someone else the right to vote on your behalf would do you any good.

No, it won't! People must take responsibility for their own votes, and look after their own interests, because others will look after their own interests first, and then maybe, if it doesn't conflict with their interests, act to protect those of others.

The solution was as obvious as the people were Oblivious to it: do away with Preemption.

But it was allowed to remain on the books, and this law was made stronger and stronger by the Pressure Pointers.

The result was that beekeepers opened their hives more and more often to find that the bees had failed to return home, having foraged in yards and fields that had been treated and sprayed with poison, and that they had no legal recourse to stop it.

There were rallies and speeches and classes held, but without the right to petition the government against Pestitution, the beekeepers found themselves at a dead end.

The national laws of Oblivion provided a right to petition the government for a redress of grievances, but the Pressure Pointers had managed to cloud the view of this right with regulations everywhere one looked.

That made it very hard to see this original, basic right, but it was still there.

Small-scale organic farming was the only safe way to grow food.

But this was not what Natural Manipulators wanted the Oblivious to do.

It wanted big agribusinesses that it could buy and control, and that would use its products.

It wanted to own the farmed food supply.

The Natural Protection Agency (NPA), the government agency of Oblivion that was responsible for tracking Potions and allowing them to be used, kept a list of Potions that it had either approved for use, was reviewing for possible use, or had banned from use. The most important part of this list, which dealt with those under review but deemed too toxic too allow for use while it was conducting its reviews, was called the Sectionate List.

Some Potions posed such clear and immediate threats to humans or to their ability to earn a living that they were immediately added to the Sectionate List. These threats included: risks to human health anywhere near the release of a Potion; risks to human health from handling the Potion during its use; risks to human health if eaten, which could happen if the Potion were used on food as it was grown; obvious harm to the environment.

The NPA worked, at least according to the laws of Oblivion, for the people of Oblivion. It was charged with preventing and remediating threats and damages to human health. The NPA presented a significant obstacle to any entity that sold Potions.

The scientists who sought to protect the honey bees and the rest of the ecosystem worked both for the NPA and at universities all around Oblivion. They published articles in peer-reviewed scientific journals that had no sales agenda, articles that were irrefutable, articles that clearly explained the damage that the potions were causing and their threat to the continued existence of the bees – all bees, not just honey bees.

They presented their findings to the Sectionate List-makers.

The problem was that the Pestituters were doing that too.

Accordingly, the NPA was lobbied heavily by Pressure-Pointers. These Pressure-Pointers were paid princely sums by BearGenics and Natural Manipulators to push the government scientists to approve all of their Potions. The Pressure-Pointers sought Exemptions to the Sectionate List. This was a Loophole that BearGenics was determined to exploit, and that was exactly what it did.

How?

Its Pressure-Pointers claimed that an unwanted insect posed such a threat to Nature – thus turning the Naturalists' argument in favor of protection against the environment and them – that the Potion under review needed to be used immediately.

Following this same argument, the Pressure-Pointers would say that an invasive insect needed to be quarantined to contain the threat it posed, so again, using the Potion would help because nothing in Nature can be contained. This argument is a fallacy, but it slipped by often.

Some insect might pose a threat to public health, another might drive farmers of a particular plant out of business if left unchecked, and so on and on unless and until the Potions under review were allowed to slip in under this Loophole.

As if that weren't enough, the Potionists of BearGenics and Natural Manipulators were allowed to conduct the studies that rule-makers relied upon when making policy. The tests in these studies were done in small fields of only a couple of acres, fields which contained only one crop. Never mind that bees forage, on average, over roughly 28,000 acres!

No independent review of industry studies was conducted. That wasn't part of NPA policy, nor did it have access to sufficient funds or resources to conduct larger studies. Thus, on the basis of these brief and tiny monoculture studies, the NPA was expected to either approve or deny permission to use whatever potions the Pestituters wanted to sell.

Clearly, the Natural Protection Agency did not live up to its name. How could it?

The insufficient funding it suffered from was caused by the politicians whose campaigns had been paid for in large part by BearGenics and Natural Manipulators.

It wasn't enough that the NPA scientists, many of whom were entomologists, were experts in their field and knew what was best for the environment and what would poison it. They needed time and money for more studies, and they needed tighter rule-making authority to block use of potions unless and until all tests showed that the bees would be safe. They didn't have it.

The NPA needed help from people who knew how to talk and write, and who would not be intimidated by questions asked in a public forum and watched by millions of witnesses on television, or by questions from the Judges of the High Court in the Marble City. They didn't have that, either.

Several of the Judges on the High Court had worked for BearGenics earlier in their careers, when they were still lawyers. The Code of Conduct for Judges required them to recuse themselves – not participate in – any case that involved BearGenics. But, they often refused to do this, and insisted upon sitting for arguments and ruling on those cases.

With these obstacles, many Potions made it past the NPA and into use.

In short, the NPA and Nature needed what they didn't have: great lawyers, fair jurists, and a decent chance of effectiveness and survival.

Engineered Static

The Observers had a problem whenever they interviewed the Thieves.

The Thieves would lie to them – not unexpected – and withhold data that did not suit their own agenda. A lie can be done by omission, by twisting facts to make untrue statements that confuse the listener, and by presenting only part of the truth while declining to mention the part that would damage that agenda.

Another method was of time lags as licenses to obliviousness, meaning that a Thief would claim that he or she could not recall a particular fact if that fact, when mentioned by an Observer, did not support the case that the Thief wished to make.

When confronted with irrefutable fact, a Thief would simply claim to have seen whatever report, and that few conclusions could be drawn from it – regardless of how well-supported it actually was.

Next, the Thief would lie with a perfectly straight face: "Our company is committed to biodiversity and to protecting pollinators." The Thieves offered various renditions of this version, but the lie was basically the same each time.

The Observer would have to content herself with getting that interchange on camera to present to the viewers, and offer comments and observations about what was missing and unanswered after the fact.

That wasn't the only problem the Observers had with the Thieves.

It didn't matter how responsible the Observers were in their efforts at news coverage or how neutral their journalistic presentations were, how well-researched and balanced. And the Observers worked very hard: they traveled all over the nation of Oblivion and to other nations, met with scientists of all academic disciplines, scientists from universities, government laboratories, and even the Potionists who worked for the Thieves. All but the Potionists were truthful with the Observers.

The Observers met with beekeepers and farmers, too.

They found out all of the things that I have told you about. They dutifully informed the people of Oblivion of the full details, in writing – on the Internet in and in print – and via other media, which included radio, television, documentaries, and also the Internet. Cyberspace, the medium of computers connected to communications networks, offered opportunities to read, to listen, to watch, and to watch and listen.

But...the Thieves had their own presentations to make.

They had their own channel on television, radio, and the Internet.

It was called Engineered Static.

They hired people to pose as Observers on it, but these individuals were no journalists.

They were puppets. They were all attractive to look at, which was one method of many for distracting their viewers. These were the newscasters, the people who simply read whatever story had been written for them to present. For interviewers, another method was used: they would simply shout down any guest who presented facts on the opposing side of the issue.

To the broadcasters of Engineered Static, science, like politics, was debatable, not an objective fact that stayed true regardless of whether or not one liked that fact.

There were some citizens of Oblivion, educated ones who read and listened to and watched the Observers very carefully. These people were trained in spotting lies and deception, and they cared about Nature and the future of the environment. They were concerned about the future of the human food supply.

The problem was that there were too few of such people.

Yes, they watched Engineered Static and discussed the lies and bullying that went on over its broadcasts, but they lacked the financial resources to effectively fight it.

The comedians of Oblivion did their best to combat the nonsense that Engineered Static was feeding the public by making fun of its broadcasts and interviews. One of them did a particularly good job of it by inviting a particularly rude interviewer onto his talk show, studying the latest issues and arguments assiduously, and then reducing him to silence with the facts.

The comedian didn't have to shout or jeer at the interviewer. The facts did the work for him.

It was not enough.

Why, when confronted by irrefutable scientific facts, had the corporations been so unyielding about making the slightest change to their policies, practices, and decisions?

It came down to one thing: money.

They would not accept anything that caused the slightest interruption or decrease to the flow of money into their coffers.

Coffers…money coffins!

Resources were boiled down to money, funneled into corporations, and then, like a black hole in space, not allowed out again. The corporations grew like monsters, choking off other areas of existence, human and otherwise.

Honey bees and other species of bees suffered and died off.

Workers got poisoned, and they sickened and died, too.

As the corporations of Thieves grew, they amassed more money – a fictitious concept, which Oblivion did not back up with any tangible asset such as gold (it had stopped that long ago). As this was done, people outside of the corporations had less and less of it with which to pay for their own survival, let alone happiness. They had so little of it that they could not pay to fight it.

Everything in human society had been organized around money to the extent that it drove every decision. There can be too much of anything, good or bad, and this was an instance of too much being focused on money.

Scaling back on decisions about honey bees that were driven by money was another factor that was killing them. The irony of this, however, was completely lost of the Thieves that drove the corporations.

But that is precisely the point: once the bees were all dead, there would be no more food for humans to eat.

And you can't eat money.

We're in So Much Trouble

When I think of the honey bees, I feel sick with dread.

We humans are an invasive species, using up and manipulating the genomes of plants like there is no tomorrow. But there will be a tomorrow, and there will be many more after it.

Whether or not they are healthy and livable, let alone bearable, is now terribly uncertain.

Those Potionists were stupid geniuses.

They thought that they were so clever, so creative...but they were idiots.

They "created" the honey bees to extinction.

I wish this were a science fiction story.

I really wish that...but it's real. What are we going to do without the honey bees?

We don't yet have nanobotic technology that is sophisticated enough to do the bees' job and pollinate the plants.

How are we going to get fruits, vegetables, and flowers to grow?

What will pollinate them?

How are we going to survive now that genetically engineered plants have multiplied and taken over the farmlands of our continent?

Without the foods that we need to have healthy, balanced nutrition, we will sicken and die.

We're in so much trouble.

We did this to ourselves.

What has been going on is like having the bear guard the beehive.

It makes no sense, because no one is watching the bear.

Sure, we know subconsciously that the bear is there doing this, but we allow other distractions to divert our attention. We choose this, and we bear responsibility for this.

It is up to us to decide which outcome we will experience – death or life.

Time is running out.

The bee death rate is too high for the species to survive.

The End: Suicide by Insecticides

In the end, the Thieves found that they had worked so hard at not having to work hard – at not having to deal naturally with insects – that nothing would grow at all.

It wouldn't grow because the soil and the bees were dead, and the very plants that required the assistance of bees to grow were toxic to them.

It was an ecological disaster of a sort and scale never seen before on the planet.

It affected every nation, because laws to stop this had been too slow to save it, and because the pestituted seeds of BearGenics had blown and grown all over Oblivion.

Too much study and proof had been required just to believe that there was a problem.

That delay had done irreparable damage.

Now the human species, along with every other species that required fruits, vegetables, and grains to survive, was paying a horrific price. No one from any other nation would approach Oblivion. It was utter chaos and misery there.

No one could grow food, so there was mass starvation. Resource wars were waged to gain access to and control of whatever food stores remained. Money didn't help. You can't eat money, and although the Thieves had hoarded enormous sums of it in accounts that they called hedge funds, there was no food to buy.

Soon societies everywhere were regressing to primitive behaviors of the sort that had been thought to be a thing of the past, only to be read about in history books. Crime was rampant, and people lived on instinct alone as they tried to survive just a little bit longer.

Some people tried to stay locked up with books and music, hoping to wait out the chaos.

Other people armed themselves with knives, guns, and whatever else they could grab and went out among others, behaving much like ancient hunters and gatherers, but in modern surroundings such as cities full of skyscrapers and suburban towns filled with strip malls and national franchises.

It was eerie to see them on the news, until the news was unable to continue broadcasting due to the hunger and desperation of the Observers themselves. What people who watched the news saw was other people dressed just like themselves, acting like lunatics and non-sentient animals, beating, maiming, and killing one another to get cans, boxes, bags, and sacks of food anywhere they could find it.

After that, there was nothing to do but wait for the end.

Some people tried to delay it by eating very little, which was possible if they lived in rural areas…for a while. But others always found them and took whatever they had away from them.

Most people just fought for whatever food they could find and died doing that.

Soon the planet was rid of the problem of humans, and able to start the natural process of healing itself.

This process takes millions of years.

Natural selection – a form of mutation – eventually healed the plants. The ones with the potions in their genetic structure died off, and the bees that lived deep in the forests were able to pollinate the remaining plants safely.

Those who benefitted from this were the creatures who lived in the wild – not humans or their domesticated pets. Many cats and dogs, formerly beloved pets who had trusted their human caregivers, had been eaten during the desperate time as the human species came to an end. Those who remained had to learn to live in the wild. Some made it, others didn't.

Humans weren't around to see that the Earth would do just fine without them, but it did.

The End: The Bees Are Saved

There is another way – another ending that is actually happy for humans.

We change our ways and save the bees. Here is how it would go:

After a few decades of politeness and trying to negotiate, the beekeepers and scientists (that is to say, the scientists who didn't work for huge corporations) decided to go to court and sue for the right to heard, noticed, and taken seriously.

It was about time.

The beekeepers and scientists of Fleur-de-Lis had set such an excellent example and precedent that this seemed like the clearest path to salvation, and the most logical one. Thus motivated, they proceeded to press their own case in the land of Oblivion.

They won!

Farmers and big agribusinesses stopped using fertilizers, herbicides, insecticides, and fungicides. They stopped calling insecticides pesticides, finally recognizing them for what they are: indiscriminate killers of all life, not merely their intended targets.

Without these noxious chemicals, farmers finally made a choice that changed the character of the land that they worked. They chose to raise more than just two crops per acre, and they chose to grow cover crops at the end of each growing season.

The cover crops were left in place to rot, just as dead leaves do in the forest. In the spring, the farmers would not churn up the topsoil, which had been killing it, depriving it of moisture by drying it out, exposing earthworms to predatory birds, and causing a necessity for those fertilizers to be artificially introduced into the fields.

Instead of that, the farmers drove different machines over the cover crops, which were interspersed with weeds, machines with small spikes that made holes in the soil. These holes trapped rainwater, which moistened the soil and kept it that way.

The result was greater crop yields and the preservation of the Earth's topsoil.

At last, a sensible, inexpensive method, one that had been practiced by only a few farmers, was being practiced by all.

What had happened?

For one thing, the chemicals had been outlawed.

The politicians who were the minions of BearGenics and Natural Manipulators were unable to stop this. Enough of them had been voted out of office that no matter how much those corporations paid their Pressure-Pointers, there were too few minions to swing the outcome their way. The Naturalists won at last.

For another, the majority of farmers had stopped looking at the few who were using this cover-crop method and benefitting from it as odd.

Still another factor played an important role: the beekeepers stopped trying to make a living by trucking their hives across Oblivion. They no longer cared about keeping the honey bees working non-stop, without time to build up their honey stores, rest, raise new brood, and do what came naturally to them. Instead of making life with the bees all about what humans wanted from them, they decided to make life with the bees all about observing the bees and assisting them in any way that they could, regardless of outside demands on them.

This majority had decided that it could no longer afford to kill its source of income, which was Nature. Nature gives us many wonderful things:

1. Topsoil full of nutrients made from decaying plants, rainwater, groundwater, and a myriad of insects and worms, all of which make up a crucial biosystem that are necessary to grow anything;

2. Plants that can produce food and clothing, such as oranges, raspberries, peaches, carrots, tomatoes, garlic, onions, corn, wheat, okra, and cotton; and

3. Honey bees of many species, each of which focuses its efforts on a different plant, thus pollinating it and making it grow these foods, and honey of seemingly endless varieties.

Farmers, agribusinesses, and politicians had at last realized that they could not expect to go on taking from Nature without respecting it and giving back to it. Rather than wait for the proof that natural is best in the demise of the bees and then of the humans who would inevitably follow, logic took over. Long-term planning became the rule of decision-making.

We humans have only been on the Earth for an eon or so, yet it took our species just a century or two to nearly kill what took Nature billions of years to evolve. Finally, we asked ourselves why we weren't more careful. Why?!

You know why. I said it at the beginning. Here it is again:

Entrusting our environment and its safety and integrity to chemicals, and stressing the elements that keep us healthy to the brink of extinction, is like leaving the bear guarding the beehive.

Appendices of Antidotes

After reading the two possible outcomes of this situation – this idiocy of leaving the bear guarding the beehive – you might like some details as to what else the Oblivious might have done differently.

In the disaster ending, it was too late.

In the happy ending, they did have time to do these things, and so they made changes.

They didn't have to wait for the politicians and scientists to stop the Thieves.

There are some things that they could be doing right now to save the honey bees.

Appendix – Beekeeping in Cities

One thing that the people of Oblivion who live in its cities might do to save the honey bees and continue to be able to enjoy honey would be to keep beehives.

There are empty lots with soil that could be used to grow gardens of fruits, vegetables, and flowers – as long as they remove the soil first, and dig deep to remove industrial contaminants from the factories of long ago – and beehives would make a nice addition to those areas.

Rooftops are another option.

A city-dweller in an apartment or a condominium typically lives in a building with a shared rooftop. Also, people in the older parts of Oblivion's cities lived in historic houses, which had flat rooftops. There is plenty of room for a collection of potted plants up there, and for beehives.

Bee on an iris.

Another option, suggested by scientists, is to truck in soil from the countryside, carry it up to these rooftops, seed it with clover and grass – a mixture rather than a monocrop – and to plant gardens of herbs, flowers, and other crops. Beehives could be placed up there as well.

Appendix – Home Gardens for Honey Bees

A similar idea to the rooftop gardens of cities is to expand the home gardens of suburban towns and rural areas.

Instead of relying on grocery stores for one's entire food supply, the people of Oblivion could learn how to grow their own herbs, fruits, and vegetables. Lawns are a waste of water anyway. If people wanted to run and play on a lawn, they could go to a park, or maintain one area for a neighborhood to share.

It would be far better to have locally grown crops within walking distance, and to learn how to preserve them for the cold months of the year.

It would also be great to have all sorts of fresh herbs to cook with.

Each yard could grow whatever the people in the house chose, and each neighborhood could, if desired, coordinate a sharing system of whatever crops each resident chose.

There could be several different things growing outside each home, but even so, there would still be some things that a resident would want to eat but not have the room to grow. This problem could be solved not only by a grocery store or farmer's market but also by a food-sharing system.

And, of course, each home – or, if not each home, each neighborhood – could keep bees.

Why not?

Beekeepers all over Oblivion had websites, on which they sold supplies, offered beekeeping advice, published articles written in plain, simple language with photographs and easy-to-read charts and graphs, with blogs and telephone numbers.

Accessing advice would not be difficult.

All that the people of Oblivion needed was the will to try.

Appendix – Small, Diversified Crops

This part would likely be the most difficult: small, diversified crops on farms.

The difficulty is with the Thieves, because they would be loath to loosen their vise-like grip on vast tracts of land that they had possessed in one hostile takeover after another from small family farmers all over Oblivion.

The effects of this damaging attack on the food supply system had been apparent for a few decades in Oblivion's universities as agricultural schools lost funding, leaving students who wished to become farmers out of luck as they sought the prerequisite education for that career.

It had been apparent in other areas, too.

Farmers were run out of business by BearGenics seeds that blew onto their land.

The farmers also lost their assets in the economic meltdown caused by the banksters as their debts came due – debts that held exponential interest rates that they could never hope to pay.

The children of Oblivion's farmers saw what their parents went through and found other careers, other fields of study, and anything to do that kept them from having to deal with such personal calamities.

In other words, the Thieves would have to be dealt with first.

Get them, the major obstacle to change, out of the way first and there is hope.

Restructure the financial, legal, political, and regulatory systems.

Show the next generation that farming is a viable career, or could be.

Then leave it up to farmers to grow several different crops on their land at once, with beehives placed in a nearby field that is allowed to rest every few seasons. The farmers would need to refuse Potions and instead preserve topsoil by grinding the remains of their food-bearing plants to compost after each harvest, and build it back up again.

This could work.

It's not that no one knows what to do to save the food supply and the honey bees.

It's that people must be persuaded to focus so much of their attention on effecting a hugely significant change in the way that they live.

Appendix – Voting with Forks

The people of Oblivion wonder how they would ever enforce their will upon the Thieves.

The task seems impossible because the Thieves control so much money and have amassed so much influence and land where food is grown.

How could the rest of Oblivion every hope to stand up to them and get Potion-free foods?

Vote.

Don't just vote whenever there is an election, or a petition to sign.

No – they would have to vote with their forks and with their wallets.

They would have to be the opposite of Oblivious, paying attention to everything that they do.

But they could do it.

Glossary of Terms

Beekeeper A human being who works closely with honey bees, maintaining frames for a beehive to inhabit, harvesting honey as the hive is able to produce it, and worrying over and watching the health of the hive.

Beeswax A natural wax that honey bees produce in their hives. It is used as a building material for hexagonal cells to hold honey in place and house larvae.

Drone A male bee. Beehives don't produce very many drones, and the drones don't live long. They mate with a queen bee, and die immediately upon doing so.

Honey A sweet food, made by bees from the nectar they extract from flowers.

Honey Bee An insect that humans have come to depend on for pollination of crops such as fruits, nuts, and flowers. It was imported nearly four centuries ago to enable the humans who moved across the ocean in between continents to continue to enjoy the same foods that they enjoyed before the move.

Honeycomb A mass of hexagonal (6-sided) cells that honey bees build in their nests to house to their larvae, pollen, and honey.

Insecticide A poisonous chemical used to kill insects. Use of an insecticide does not allow the user to choose which insects are killed. Any that it contacts are affected.

Mites   Insects that invade beehives, enter cells, and attach themselves to larvae and bees, and weaken their hosts.

Nectar   A sugar-rich liquid that flowering plants produce as a lure to pollen-carrying insects such as bees.

Neonicotinoid   A class of insecticides that affect the neurological system of any insect or animal that comes in contact with it.

Nosema   A mold that infests the intestines of bees.

Pollen   A fine, coarse, powder that contains the gametes – genetic material – of plants.

Propolis   A resinous mixture from sap flows, tree sap, and other sources. Bees use propolis for sealing off the hive against mites, intruders, and decaying intruders.

Queen Bee   A female bee that is grown with extra royal jelly in her larval cell. She lives 2 to 3 years, and makes one virgin flight upon growing to full size, which is larger than the other bees. On that flight, she mates with as many drones as possible, then stores the genetic material that she gathers so that she may then spend the rest of her life constantly laying eggs...and doing nothing other than that and eating.

Royal Jelly   A substance secreted by honey bees that is used as nutrition for larvae and adult queen bees. Extra royal jelly is fed to larvae that worker bees have chosen to become queen bees. This causes ovaries to fully develop in those larvae.

Supersedure The replacement of an aging, ailing queen bee by worker bees, done when the queen bee's pheromone levels decrease. This tells the worker bees that it is time to grow replacements. Only one is needed, but many are created. The new queen bees immediately fight for dominance. The last one alive wins.

Worker Bee A female bee that is one of the majority of the bees in a hive. She does not reproduce, but instead spends her entire life working at a variety of jobs both in and outside of the hive: scout, nurse, nectar gatherer, pollen gatherer, queen bee attendant.

Bibliography

Scientific Articles

1. Margaret Tuttle McGrath, 2004. "What are Fungicides?" *The Plant Health Instructor* DOI: 10.1094/PHI-I-2004-0825-01. *American Phytopathological Society.* Online at http://www.apsnet.org/edcenter/intropp/topics/Pages/Fungicides.aspx

2. Randy Oliver, 2007. IPM7 – The Arsenal: "Natural" Treatments – Part 2. *Scientific Beekeeping.* Online at http://scientificbeekeeping.com/ipm-7-the-arsenal-natural-treatments-part-2/

3. Randy Oliver, February 2011. Miticides. *American Bee Journal* and *Scientific Beekeeping.* Online at http://scientificbeekeeping.com/miticides-2011/

4. Johnson RM, Dahlgren L, Siegfried BD, Ellis MD, 2013. Acaricide, Fungicide and Drug Interactions in Honey Bees (*Apis mellifera*). *PLoS ONE* 8(1): e54092. doi:10.1371/journal.pone.0054092. Online at http://www.plosone.org/article/info%3Adoi%2F10.1371%2Fjournal.pone.0054092

5. Lundgren, Jonathan G. and Duan, Jian J. August 2013. RNAi-Based Insecticidal Crops: Potential Effects on Nontarget Species. *BioScience* 63: 657–665. doi:10.1525/bio.2013.63.8.8. ISSN 0006-3568, electronic ISSN 1525-3244. Online at http://www.aibs.org/bioscience-press-releases/resources/Lundgren.pdf

6. M. A. Fürst, D. P. McMahon, J. L. Osborne, R. J. Paxton, and M. J. F. Brown. Disease associations between honeybees and bumblebees as a threat to wild pollinators. *Nature* 506, 364–366 (20 February 2014) doi:10.1038/nature12977. Online at http://www.nature.com/nature/journal/v506/n7488/full/nature12977.html

7. Lian JL, Cornman RS, Evans JD, Pettis JS, Zhao Y, Murphy C, Peng WJ, Wu J, Hamilton M, Boncristiani HF, Jr., Zhou L, Hammond J, Chen YP. 2014. Systemic spread and propagation

of a plant-pathogenic virus in European honeybees, *Apis mellifera. mBio* 5(1):e00898-13. doi:10.1128/mBio.00898-13.

8.   Sandrock, C., Tanadini, M., Tanadini, L.G., Fausser-Lisslin, A., Polts, S.G., and Neumann, P. Impact of chronic neonicotinoid exposure on honeybee colony performance and queen supersedure. *PLoS One.* 1 August 2014; 9(8):e103592. doi: 10.1371/journal.pone.0103592. eCollection 2014.

News Articles

9.   *EuroNews High-Tech*: "No Bees No Fruits," *YourIS.com/European Research Media Center*, 21 November 2007, online at http://www.youris.com/Environment/GLOBALCHANGETV/No_Bees_No_Fruits.kl

10.   Sergio Pistoi, "Bee mortality has never been so high all over the world at the same time," *YourIS.com/European Research Media Center*, 20 May 2009, online at http://www.youris.com/Environment/Bees/Bee_mortality_has_never_be_so_high_all_over_the_world_at_the_same_time.kl

11.   "World relies on endangered bees for 153 billion euros," *YourIS.com/European Research Media Center*, 20 May 2009, online at http://www.youris.com/Environment/Bees/World_relies_on_endangered_bees_for_153_billion_euros.kl

12.   Sergio Pistoi, "Bees go mad and become lost because of neonicotinoid dispersion," *YourIS.com/European Research Media Center*, 1 June 2009, online at http://www.youris.com/Environment/Bees/Bees_go_mad_and_become_lost_because_of_neonicotinoid_dispersion.kl

13.   Sergio Pistoi, "Bees 'restored to health' in Italy after this spring's neonicotinoid-free maize sowing," *YourIS.com/European Research Media Center*, 6 June 2009, online at http://www.youris.com/Environment/Bees/Bees_restored_to_he

alth_in_Italy_after_this_springs_neonicotinoidfree_maize_sowi
ng.kl

14. *The Independent*: "Bees take flight to the city after fall in rural hive numbers," *YourIS.com/European Research Media Center*, 1 March 2010, online at http://www.youris.com/Picked_Up/Bees_take_flight_to_the_city _after_fall_in_rural_hive_numbers.kl

15. *Science Daily*: "Microbial Team May Be Culprit in Colony Collapse Disorder," *YourIS.com/European Research Media Center*, 27 May 2010, online at http://www.youris.com/Picked_Up/MicrobialTeamMayBeCulpri tInColonyCollapseDisorder.kl

16. *News.Scotsman.com*: "Scientists get £1.8 million to study effects of pesticides on bees' brains," *YourIS.com/European Research Media Center*, 22 June 2010, online at http://www.youris.com/Picked_Up/Scientists_To_Get_18m_To_ Study_Effect_Of_Pesticides_On_Bees_Brains.kl

17. Kirk Johnson, "Possible Cause of Bee Die-Off is Found," *The New York Times*, 7 October 2010, page A1, online at http://www.nytimes.com/2010/10/07/science/07bees.html?hp

18. Sarah C. Corriher, "The Bees Are Dying and How Monsanto Will Be Responsible for the Upcoming Famine," *The Health Wyze Report*, 8 October 2010, online at http://healthwyze.org/index.php/component/content/article/498- the-bees-are-dying-and-how-monsanto-will-be-responsible-for- the-upcoming-famine.html

19. *Telegraph*: "Study finds causes of Colony Collapse Disorder in bees," *YourIS.com/European Research Media Center*, 11 October 2010, online at http://www.youris.com/Picked_Up/Study_Finds_Causes_Of_Co lony_Collapse_Disorder_In_Bees.kl

20. *BBC News*: "Nature's Sting: the real cost of damaging Planet Earth," *YourIS.com/European Research Media Center*, 15 October 2010, online at http://www.youris.com/Environment/Picked_for_you/NatureS_S ting_The_Real_Cost_Of_Damaging_Planet_Earth.kl

21.	Mary Ann DeSantis and John Jernigan, "Umatilla Gold," *Ocala Style*, November 2010, online at http://www.maryanndesantis.com/wp-content/uploads/2012/03/1110-UmatillaGold.pdf

22.	Jesse McKinley, "Farm Thieves Target Grapes, and Even Bees," *The New York Times*, 22 July 2011, page A1, online at http://www.nytimes.com/2011/07/22/us/22crime.html?hp=&pagewanted=all

23.	Starling Childs, "I Love my Smart Meter – It Kills Bees!" *Stop Smart Meters!* 31 October 2011, online at http://stopsmartmeters.org/2011/10/31/i-love-my-smart-meter-it-kills-bees/

24.	Esther Manilla, "Bees: The Threatened Link in Food Security," *Truthout.org*, 5 April 2012, online at http://truth-out.org/news/item/8334-bees-the-threatened-link-in-food-security

25.	Emily S. Rueb, "As Swarms Startle New York, Beekeeper Keeps Busy," *The New York Times*, 19 June 2012, page A1, online at http://www.nytimes.com/2012/06/19/nyregion/honeybee-swarms-increase-in-nyc-after-mild-spring.html

26.	Todd Corillo, "Virginia will pay you to take up beekeeping," *WTKR News – Channel 3*, 10 January 2013, online at http://wtkr.com/2013/01/10/virginia-will-pay-you-to-take-up-beekeeping/

27.	Beth Buczynski, "Why Isn't the EPA Doing Something About Bee-Killing Insecticides?" *Care2 Causes*, 21 January 2013, online at http://www.care2.com/causes/why-isnt-the-epa-doing-something-about-bee-killing-insecticides.html?cid=fb_causes_why-isnt-the-epa-doing-something-about-bee-killing-insecticides

28.	Bernhard Warner, "To Revive Honeybees, Europe Proposes a Pesticide Ban," *Bloomberg Businessweek – Very Near Future*, 19 February 2013, online at http://www.businessweek.com/articles/2013-02-19/to-revive-honey-bees-europe-proposes-a-pesticide-ban

29. Beth Buczynski, "Poisoned Bees Will Get Their Day in Court," *Care2 Causes*, 14 March 2013, online at http://www.care2.com/causes/poisoned-bees-will-get-their-day-in-court.html

30. Michael Pollan, "CFS, Beekeepers and Public Interest Groups Sue EPA Over Bee-Toxic Pesticides," *Center for Food Safety*, March 21, 2013, online at http://www.centerforfoodsafety.org/press-releases/1911/cfs-beekeepers-and-public-interest-groups-sue-epa-over-bee-toxic-pesticides#

31. Kristina Chew, "Flowers Contaminated With Metal Behind Bumblebee Decline," *Care2 Causes*, 6 April 2013, online at http://www.care2.com/causes/flowers-contaminated-with-metal-behind-bumblebee-decline.html#ixzz2PiLwEVTN

32. Alexis Baden-Mayer, "A shocking number of children have never seen a bee," *Bee the Change*, 15 April 2013, online at http://www.causes.com/actions/1746684-a-shocking-number-of-children-have-never-seen-a-bee?open_dialog=inviter&recruiter_id=344643&utm_campaign=activity_mailer%2Fnew_activity&utm_medium=email&utm_source=causes&token=ukCz4rd-luFm2Jll8HCVRfvP

33. Geoffrey Mohan, "High-Fructose Corn Syrup Linked to Bee Colony Collapse," *The Los Angeles Times*, 29 April 2013, in Honey Colony, 13 May 2013, online at http://www.honeycolony.com/article/high-fructose-corn-syrup-linked-to-bee-colony-collapse/

34. Sergio Pistoi, "Marco Lodesani: Lessons learned from the Italian ban on pesticides," *YourIS.com/European Research Media Center*, 2 May 2013, online at http://www.youris.com/Environment/Interviews/Marco_Lodesani_Lessons_From_The_Italian_Ban_On_Pesticides.kl

35. Anthony King, "Bees survival: ban more pesticides?" *YourIS.com/European Research Media Center*, 2 May 2013, online at

http://www.youris.com/Environment/Bees/Bees_Survival_Ban_More_Pesticides.kl

36. Jennifer S. Holland, "The Plight of the Honeybee," *National Geographic News*, 10 May 2013, online at http://news.nationalgeographic.com/news/2013/13/130510-honeybee-bee-science-european-union-pesticides-colony-collapse-epa-science/?rptregcta=reg_free_np&rptregcampaign=20131004_rw_membership_n2p_us_w#

37. FoodFreedomGroup.com: "Illinois Illegal Seizes Bees Resistant to Monsanto's Roundup, Killing remaining Queens," *Global Research*, 24 May 2013, online at http://www.globalresearch.ca/illinois-illegally-seizes-bees-resistant-to-monsantos-roundup-kills-remaining-queens/5336210

38. "Monsanto's Campaign Contributions to US House and Senate Candidates," *Global Research News*, 26 May 2013, online at http://www.globalresearch.ca/monsantos-contributions-to-us-house-and-senate-candidates/5336404

39. Staff, "Bear disturbs beehive in East Amwell, resident reports," *Hunterdon County Democrat*, 6 June 2013, online at http://www.nj.com/hunterdon-county-democrat/index.ssf/2013/06/your_photos_bear_claw_marks_da.html

40. Alison Benjamin, "Third of all honeybee colonies in England did not survive winter," *The Guardian*, 12 June 2013, online at http://www.guardian.co.uk/environment/2013/jun/13/honeybee-colonies-england-winter

41. Cassandra Profita, "Xerxes Society: Wilsonville Bees Died from Pesticide Poisoning," *OPB*, 19 June 2013, online at http://www.opb.org/news/blog/ecotrope/xerces-society-wilsonville-bees-died-from-pesticide-poisoning/

42. Scott Helman, "The Bee Keepers: The Harvard Scientist Linking Pesticides to Honeybee Colony Collapse Disorder," *The Boston Globe*, 23 June 2013, online at http://www.bostonglobe.com/magazine/2013/06/22/the-harvard-

scientist-linking-pesticides-honeybee-colony-collapse-disorder/nXvIA5I6IcxFRxEOc8tpFI/story.html

43.   John Upton, "Buzzkill: Huge bee die-off in Oregon parking lot blamed on insecticide spraying," *Grist*, 20 June 2013, online at http://grist.org/news/huge-bee-die-off-in-oregon-parking-lot-blamed-on-insecticide-spraying/?utm_campaign=weekly&utm_medium=email&utm_source=newsletter&sub_email=katherine%40organicconsumers.org

44.   Heather Dewar, "Study Shows Common Chemicals Harm Honey Bees' Health," *UMD Right Now*, 24 June 2013, online at http://umdrightnow.umd.edu/news/study-shows-common-chemicals-harm-honey-bees-health

45.   "Italian farm minister pushes for GM crop ban," *Farming Online*, 25 June 2013, online at http://www.farming.co.uk/news/article/8548

46.   Devin Kelly, "Oregon temporarily restricts pesticide use following bee deaths," *Los Angeles Times*, 27 June 2013, online at http://www.latimes.com/news/nation/nationnow/la-na-nn-oregon-pesticides-restricted-20130626,0,3014501.story

47.   Matt McDermott, "Bee Colonies are Dying from Non-Lethal Fungicides," *Motherboard*, July 2013, online at http://motherboard.vice.com/blog/bee-colonies-are-dying-from-non-lethal-fungicides

48.   Michele Colopy and Liz Judge, "Beekeeping Industry Sues EPA for Approval of Bee-Killing Pesticide," *Earth Justice*, 8 July 2013, online at http://earthjustice.org/news/press/2013/beekeeping-industry-sues-epa-for-approval-of-bee-killing-pesticide

49.   Ann Werner, "When All the Bees Are Gone, How Will We Survive?" *Liberals Unite*, 15 July 2013, online at http://samuel-warde.com/2013/07/when-all-the-bees-are-gone-how-will-we-survive/

50. Defenders of Wildlife, "Talk about a Buzzkill," *Wild Matters*, Summer 2013, online at http://www.defenders.org/magazine/summer-2013/wild-matters

51. Judy Benson, "The Importance of Bee-ing: Pollination Focus of State Research," *The Hartford Courant* and *The Day, McClatchy-Tribune News Service*, 18 July 2013, online at http://articles.courant.com/2013-07-18/news/hc-bees-new-research-pesticides-20130715_1_wild-bees-honey-bees-mark-creighton

52. Rebekah Marcarelli, "Bumblebees Return; Rare Species' Reemergence in Washington Leaves Scientists 'Giddy'," *HNGN: Headlines & Global News*, 22 July 2013, online at http://www.hngn.com/articles/8306/20130722/bumblebees-return-rare-species-reemergence-washington-leaves-scientists-giddy-photo.htm

53. Nicole Ostrow, "Honeybee Health Damaged by Common Fungicides, Study Finds," *Bloomberg News*, 24 July 2013, online at http://www.bloomberg.com/news/2013-07-24/honeybee-health-damaged-by-common-fungicides-study-finds.html

54. Kim Kaplan, "Bees Exposed to Fungicide More Vulnerable to Nosema Parasite," *USDA*, 24 July 2013, online at http://www.ars.usda.gov/is/pr/2013/130724.htm

55. Willy Blackmore, "Colony Collapse Disorder: It's Complicated," *Take Part*, 25 July 2013, online at http://www.takepart.com/article/2013/07/25/colony-collapse-disorder-its-complicated

56. Candy Thomson, "Pesticides, fungicides harming bee colonies, UM study says," *The Baltimore Sun*, 26 July 2013, online at http://articles.baltimoresun.com/2013-07-26/features/bs-md-bee-death-study-20130726_1_pollen-um-study-nosema

57. Richard Gray, "Radar Antennae Reveal How Disease and Pesticides are Harming Bees Navigation," *The Telegraph*, 28 July 2013, online at http://www.telegraph.co.uk/gardening/beekeeping/10206225/Ra

dar-antennae-reveal-how-disease-and-pesticides-are-harming-bees-navigation.html

58. Staff Compilation, "Bees Exposed to Fungicide More Vulnerable to Gut Parasite, USDA Says," *Farm Futures*, 29 July 2013, online at http://farmfutures.com/story-bees-exposed-fungicide-more-vulnerable-gut-parasite-usda-says-0-100780

59. Tom Philpott, "The Mystery of Bee Colony Collapse," *Mother Jones*, 31 July 2013, online at http://www.motherjones.com/tom-philpott/2013/07/bee-colony-collapse-disorder-fungicides

60. Matthew Charles Cardinale, "Bill Seeks to Halt Bee-Killing Pesticides in U.S.," *Nation of Change*, 31 July 2013, online at http://www.nationofchange.org/bill-seeks-halt-bee-killing-pesticides-us-1375280634

61. Elizabeth Kucinich, "The Killing Fields: Industrial Agriculture, Dead Zones and Genetically Engineered Corn," *The Huffington Post*, 1 August 2013, online at http://www.huffingtonpost.com/elizabeth-kucinich/the-killing-fields-indust_b_3678515.html

62. Maryam Henein, "Bees Dying by the Millions as Colony Collapse Accelerates," *HoneyColony*, 8 August 2013, online at http://www.honeycolony.com/article/bees-dying-by-the-millions/

63. Megan McGrath, "Plant Fungicide Might Hurt Honeybees," *Voice of America*, 9 August 2013, online at http://www.voanews.com/content/fungicide--for-plants-may-hurt-honeybees/1727174.html

64. Bryan Walsh, The Trouble with Beekeeping in the Anthropocene, *Time*, 9 August 2013, online at http://science.time.com/2013/08/09/the-trouble-with-beekeeping-in-the-anthropocene/

65. Clare Leschin-Hoar, "Are Your 'Bee-Friendly' Garden Plants Actually Killing Bees?" *Take Part*, 14 August 2013, online at http://www.takepart.com/article/2013/08/14/your-bee-friendly-garden-killing-bees

66. Erich Pica, "Gardeners Beware: "Bee-friendly Plants May Be Poisoning Bees," *The Huffington Post*, 15 August 2013, online at http://www.huffingtonpost.com/erich-pica/gardeners-beware-beefrien_b_3757020.html

67. Bryan Walsh, "The Plight of the Honeybee," *Time*, 19 August 2013, online at http://time.com/559/the-plight-of-the-honeybee/

68. Katherine Boughton, "Connecticut No Land for Honeybees," *Litchfield County Times*, 23 August 2013, online at http://www.countytimes.com/articles/2013/08/23/business/doc52161bb1cda06770952892.txt?viewmode=fullstory

69. Jen Hayden, "Florida citrus grower gets slap on the wrist after killing millions of honeybees," *Daily Kos*, 29 August 2013, online at http://www.dailykos.com/story/2013/08/29/1234812/-Florida-citrus-grower-gets-slap-on-the-wrist-after-killing-millions-of-honeybees?detail=facebook#

70. Dr. Mercola, "Home Gardeners Beware: Tests Reveal Many Garden Plants Are Treated with Bee-Killing Pesticides," *Friends of the Earth* and *Dr. Mercola*, 3 September 2013, online at http://action.foe.org/p/dia/action3/common/public/?action_KEY=14141 and http://articles.mercola.com/sites/articles/archive/2013/09/03/garden-plants-pesticides.aspx

71. Tom Philpott, "One Weird Trick to Fix Farms Forever," *Mother Jones*, 9 September 2013, online at http://www.motherjones.com/environment/2013/09/cover-crops-no-till-david-brandt-farms

72. Sayer Ji, "Study Links Roundup 'Weedkiller' to Overgrowth of Deadly Fungal Toxins ," *GreenMedInfo*, 9 September 2013, online at http://www.greenmedinfo.com/blog/breaking-study-links-roundup-weedkiller-overgrowth-deadly-fungal-toxins-1

73. Canadian Honey Council, "Pioneer offers neonicotinoid-free corn, soybean seed in Canada," *AG Professional*, 12 September 2013, online at http://www.agprofessional.com/news/Pioneer-offers-neonicotinoid-free-corn-soybean-seed-in-Canada-223447931.html

74. Cornucopia Institute, "Canada Declares Farm Use of Neonicotinoids "Unsustainable"," *CBC* and *Health Canada*, 18 September 2013, online at http://www.cornucopia.org/2013/09/canada-declares-farm-use-neonicotinoids-unsustainable/

75. Susan Berfield, "The Honey Launderers: Uncovering the Largest Food Fraud in U.S. History," *Bloomberg Businessweek*, 23 September 2013, online at http://finance.yahoo.com/news/the-honey-launderers--uncovering-the-largest-food-fraud-in-u-s--history-171454285.html

76. Laurene Williams, "What Filmmaker Jeremy Seifert Told Me About the Politics of Health," *HoneyColony Original*, 28 September 2013, online at http://www.honeycolony.com/article/gmo-omg-a-conversation-with-jeremy-seifert-on-the-politics-of-health-and-biotech-foods/

77. Jenna Blumenfeld, "Why you should care about GMOs," *Delicious Living*, 30 September 2013, online at http://deliciousliving.com/health/why-you-should-care-about-gmos?page=1

78. Helen Thompson, "Fuel Exhaust Disrupts Scent Signals for Honeybees," *National Geographic*, 3 October 2013, online at http://news.nationalgeographic.com/news/energy/2013/10/131003-fuel-exhaust-scent-disrupts-signals-honeybees/

79. Beyond Pesticides, "Scientists Discover Key Molecule Linking Neonicotinoids to Honey Bee Viruses," *EcoWatch*, October 24, 2013, online at http://ecowatch.com/2013/10/24/key-molecule-links-neonicoinoids-to-bee-viruses/

80. Brian, "37 million Bees found dead in Elmwood, Ontario, Canada, after large planting of GMO corn seed treated with Neonicotinoid pesticides," *Live Free, Live Natural*, 30 October 2013, online at http://livefreelivenatural.com/37-million-bees-found-dead-elmwood-ontario-canada-large-planting-gmo-corn-seed-treated-neonicotinoid-pesticides/

81. Maryam Henein, "Long Live the Queen Bee," *HoneyColony*, 2 December 2013, online at http://www.honeycolony.com/article/long-live-the-queen-bee/

82. Christina Sarich, "India Creates Organic Seed Bank in Response to GMO Suicide Deeds, Farmer Debt," *Nation of Change*, 2 December 2013, online at http://www.nationofchange.org/india-creates-organic-seed-bank-response-gmo-suicide-seeds-farmer-debt-1385995833

83. Paul Towers, "Above the Fold: EPA, Protect Bees!" *HoneyColony*, 4 December 2013, online at http://www.honeycolony.com/article/above-the-fold-epa-protect-bees/?utm_source=HoneyColony+Contacts&utm_campaign=55 0e247161-November_4_AB11_5_2013&utm_medium=email&utm_term= 0_d9922aaff1-550e247161-57774365

84. Raviya Ismail, "Why Honeybees Matter," *Earth Justice*, 6 December 2013, online at http://earthjustice.org/blog/2013-december/why-honeybees-matter&utm_source=Convio

85. Green Right Now Reports, "Beekeepers and food and environmental groups sue EPA over pesticides toxic to bees," *PAHomepage*, 11 December 2013, online at http://www.pahomepage.com/story/d/story/beekeepers-and-food-and-environment-groups-sue-epa/40964/75GMmqa2HE2ya9id-wofpQ

86. Danny Hakim, "European Agency Warns of Risk to Humans in Pesticides Tied to Bee Deaths," *The New York Times*, 17 December 2013, online at http://www.nytimes.com/2013/12/18/business/international/europe-warns-of-human-risk-from-insecticides.html?nl=todaysheadlines&emc=edit_ee_20131218& _r=4&

87. Kendall Helblig, "EPA's system of tracking pesticides harmful to honeybees, critics say," *The Washington Post*, 22 December 2013, online at http://www.washingtonpost.com/politics/epas-system-of-tracking-pesticides-harmful-to-honeybees-critics-say/2013/12/22/7346a80c-6835-11e3-8b5b-a77187b716a3_story.html

88.   Amy Harmon, "A Lonely Quest for Facts on Genetically
      Modified Crops," *The New York Times*, 4 January 2014, online
      at http://www.nytimes.com/2014/01/05/us/on-hawaii-a-lonely-
      quest-for-facts-about-gmos.html?_r=2

89.   Michael Wines, "Bee Deaths May Stem from Virus, Study
      Says," *The New York Times*, January 21, 2014, online at
      http://www.nytimes.com/2014/01/22/us/bee-deaths-may-stem-
      from-virus-study-says.html?ref=michaelwines

90.   Maryam Henein, "10 Surprising Statistics About Honeybees,"
      Honey Colony, January 22, 2014, online at
      http://www.honeycolony.com/article/10-surprising-statistics-
      about-
      honeybees/?utm_source=HoneyColony+Contacts&utm_campaig
      n=e90a4ed9d1-
      November_4_AB11_5_2013&utm_medium=email&utm_term=
      0_d9922aaff1-e90a4ed9d1-57774365

91.   Douglas Quenqua, "New Lead in Honeybee Deaths and Another
      Hot Year on Earth," *The New York Times*, January 27, 2014,
      online at http://www.nytimes.com/2014/01/28/science/new-lead-
      in-honeybee-deaths-and-another-hot-year-on-earth.html

92.   Andrew Pollack, "Genetic Weapon Against Insects Raises Hope
      and Fear in Farming," *The New York Times*, January 27, 2014,
      online at http://www.nytimes.com/2014/01/28/business/energy-
      environment/genetic-weapon-against-insects-raises-hope-and-
      fear-in-farming.html?ref=science

93.   Beth Garbitelli, ""Zombie Bees" Invade Eastern U.S. for 1st
      Time," *NBC*, January 29, 2014, online at
      http://www.nbcconnecticut.com/news/national-
      international/NATL-Zombie-Bees-Invade-East-Coast-1st-Time-
      Beekeeper-Vermont-Anthony-Cantrell-Beehive-
      242494121.html?fb_ref=s%3DshowShareBarUI%3Ap%3Dface
      book-send&fb_source=message

94.   Maryam Henein, "Systemic Pesticides Harm Bees and (Our)
      Brains," *Honey Colony*, 4 February 2014, online at
      http://www.honeycolony.com/article/systemic-pesticides-harm-
      bees-and-our-

brains/?utm_source=HoneyColony+Contacts&utm_campaign=4
165c45c04-
November_4_AB11_5_2013&utm_medium=email&utm_term=
0_d9922aaff1-4165c45c04-57774365

95. Beyond Pesticides article, "EPA Approves Another Pesticide Highly Toxic to Bees," *EcoWatch*, 7 February 2014, online at http://ecowatch.com/2014/02/07/epa-approves-another-pesticide-toxic-bees/

96. Gregory B. Hladky, "State Falling Short in Keeping Track of Pesticide Use," *The Hartford Courant*, 19 February 2014, online at http://www.courant.com/news/politics/hc-pesticide-reports-0217-20140218,0,3363086,full.story

97. Willy Blackmore, "In the Midwest, It's Monarchs Versus Monsanto," *Take Part*, 25 February 2014, online at http://www.takepart.com/article/2014/02/25/monarchs-versus-monsanto

98. Lisa Arkin, "Eugene First City to Ban Bee-Killing Neonics," *Honey Colony*, 10 March 2014, online at http://www.honeycolony.com/article/eugene-first-city-to-ban-bee-killing-neonics/?utm_source=HoneyColony+Contacts&utm_campaign=8f88c66079-
November_4_AB11_5_2013&utm_medium=email&utm_term=
0_d9922aaff1-8f88c66079-57774365

99. Luke Garratt, "Sticky situation – The amazing honey hunters who risk their lives in the foothills of the Himalayas to collect honey from the hives of the world's largest honeybees," *Mail Online*, 19 March 2014, online at http://www.dailymail.co.uk/news/article-2584541/Sticky-situation-The-amazing-honey-hunters-risk-lives-foothills-Himalayas-collect-honey-hives-worlds-largest-honeybees.html

100. Mariah Blake, "The Scary New Evidence on BPA-Free Plastics," *Mother Jones*, March/April 2014, online at http://www.motherjones.com/environment/2014/03/tritan-certichem-eastman-bpa-free-plastic-safe

101. Wendy Park and Jay Feldman, "Health Advocates Challenge EPA's Failure to Require Pesticide Ingredient Disclosure," *Earth Justice*, 5 March 2014, online at http://earthjustice.org/news/press/2014/health-advocates-challenge-epa-s-failure-to-require-pesticide-ingredient-disclosure

102. Katherine Paul and Ronnie Cummins, "5 New Reasons Monsanto's 'Science' Doesn't Add Up," *Honey Colony*, 8 March 2014, online at http://www.honeycolony.com/article/5-new-reasons-monsantos-science-doesnt-add-up/?utm_source=HoneyColony+Contacts&utm_campaign=93f3256744-November_4_AB11_5_2013&utm_medium=email&utm_term=0_d9922aaff1-93f3256744-57774365

103. "16 Cancer Causing Foods That You Probably Eat Every Day," *Natural Foods News*, 9 March 2014, online at http://naturalon.com/10-of-the-most-cancer-causing-foods/16/

104. Kim Willsher, "French Organic Winemaker Faces Prison for Defying Pesticide Order," *The Guardian* via *The Cornucopia Institute*, 11 March 2014, online at http://www.cornucopia.org/2014/03/french-organic-winemaker-faces-prison-defying-pesticide-order

105. Jane Lear, "Make Your Garden a Sanctuary for Bees," *Take Part*, 18 March 2014, online at http://www.takepart.com/article/2014/03/18/bee-friendly-garden?cmpid=tpdaily-eml-2014-03-19

106. Claire Leschin-Hoar, "Is This the Most Bee-Friendly City in America?" *Take Part*, 18 March 2014, online at http://www.takepart.com/article/2014/03/18/bee-friendliest-city-america-eugene-oregon?cmpid=tpdaily-eml-2014-03-19

107. Larissa Walker, "Half Million Sign Bernie the Bee Petition to Save the Bees," *Honey Colony*, 21 March 2014, online at http://www.honeycolony.com/article/half-million-sign-bernie-the-bee-petition-to-save-the-bees/?utm_source=HoneyColony+Contacts&utm_campaign=9ede1d3a4f-

November_4_AB11_5_2013&utm_medium=email&utm_term=
0_d9922aaff1-9ede1d3a4f-57774365

108.   Mariah Blake, "Scientists Condemn New FDA Study Saying
       BPA Is Safe: 'It Borders on Academic Misconduct'," *Mother
       Jones*, 24 March 2014, online at
       http://www.motherjones.com/environment/2014/03/scientists-
       slam-fda-study-bpa

109.   George B. Hladky, "Pesticide Compliance: Hundreds of
       Complaints, Few Fines," *The Hartford Courant*, 24 March 2014,
       online at http://www.courant.com/news/connecticut/hc-
       pesticide-violation-enforcement-0312-
       20140321,0,1930085,full.story

110.   Honey Colony Staff, "Brazil Seeks Ban on Monsanto Herbicide
       Due to Alarming Toxicity Risks," *Honey Colony*, 2 April 2014,
       online at http://www.honeycolony.com/article/brazil-seeks-ban-
       on-monsanto-herbicide-due-to-alarming-toxicity-
       risks/?utm_source=HoneyColony+Contacts&utm_campaign=c6
       1780fe30-
       November_4_AB11_5_2013&utm_medium=email&utm_term=
       0_d9922aaff1-c61780fe30-57774365

111.   Justine Alford, "European Bumblebees Under Threat, *IFL
       Science*, 2 April 2014, online at
       http://www.iflscience.com/plants-and-animals/european-
       bumblebees-under-threat

112.   Maryam Henein, "Systemic Pesticides Kill Bees and Harm the
       Environment," *Honey Colony*, 3 April 2014, online at
       http://www.honeycolony.com/article/systemic-pesticides-kill-
       bees-harm-
       environment/?utm_source=HoneyColony+Contacts&utm_camp
       aign=c61780fe30-
       November_4_AB11_5_2013&utm_medium=email&utm_term=
       0_d9922aaff1-c61780fe30-57774365

113.   Danielle L. Davis, "How Keeping Your Food Bug-Free is
       Hurting Countless Women," *Take Part*, 9 April 2014, online at
       http://www.takepart.com/article/2014/04/09/pesticide-
       drift?cmpid=tpdaily-eml-2014-04-09

114. Zen Honeycutt and Henry Rowlands via *Sustainable Pulse*, "World's #1 Herbicide Discovered in U.S. Mothers' Breast Milk," *GreenMedInfo*, 8 April 2014, online at http://www.greenmedinfo.com/blog/world-s-1-herbicide-discovered-us-mothers-breast-milk

115. June Stoyer, "Beekeepers Discuss Mass Honeybee Deaths During Almond Pollination," *The Organic View*, 11 April 2014, online at http://www.theorganicview.com/environment/beekeepers-discuss-mass-honeybee-deaths-from-almond-pollination/

116. Laurene Williams, "Tristan Copley Smith: How DIY Beehives Can Open Solutions," *Buzzworthy Blogs* via *Honey Colony*, 17 April 2014, online at http://www.honeycolony.com/article/tristan-copley-smith-open-bee-hives-can-open-solutions/?utm_source=HoneyColonyContacts

117. Michele Simon, "Follow the Honey: 7 Ways Pesticide Companies are Spinning the Bee Crisis to Protect Profits," *Eat Drink Politics*, 27 April 2014, online at http://www.eatdrinkpolitics.com/2014/04/27/follow-the-honey-7-ways-pesticide-companies-are-spinning-the-bee-crisis-to-protect-profits/

118. Marge Dwyer, "Study strengthens link between neonicotinoids and collapse of honey bee colonies," *Harvard School of Public Health*, 9 May 2014, online at http://www.hsph.harvard.edu/news/press-releases/study-strengthens-link-between-neonicotinoids-and-collapse-of-honey-bee-colonies/

119. Jake Bova, "Study Claims Colony Collapse Disorder Caused by Insecticides," *IFL Science*, 12 May 2014, online at http://www.iflscience.com/plants-and-animals/study-claims-colony-collapse-disorder-caused-insecticides

120. Tom Philpott, "Did Scientist Just Solve the Bee Collapse Mystery?" *Mother Jones*, 20 May 2014, online at http://www.motherjones.com/tom-philpott/2014/05/smoking-gun-bee-collapse

121. Jane Lear, "Jane Says: Make Room for Birds and Butterflies in Your Garden," *Take Part*, 28 May 2014, online at http://www.takepart.com/article/2014/05/28/wildlife-garden?cmpid=tpdaily-eml-2014-05-28

122. Press Release: "One Year After GE Wheat Contamination, USDA Has Failed to Protect Farmers," *Center for Food Safety*, 29 May 2014, online at http://www.centerforfoodsafety.org/press-releases/3180/one-year-after-ge-wheat-contamination-usda-has-failed-to-protect-farmers

123. Cassius Methyl, "Report: Honeybee Death Rate is Currently Too High for Survival of the Species," *Live Free Live Natural*, 3 June 2014, online at http://livefreelivenatural.com/honeybee-death-rate-currently-high-survival-species-crucial-food/

124. Molly Redden, "Take the Honey and Run: Meet California's Most Notorious Beenapper," *Mother Jones*, 5 June 2014, online at http://www.motherjones.com/environment/2014/06/david-allred-california-bee-theft

125. Kristine Wong, "Scientists Create a Pesticide That Won't Kill the Bees – and It's All Natural," *Take Part*, 6 June 2014, online at http://www.takepart.com/article/2014/06/06/heres-pesticide-wont-kill-bees-and-its-all-natural?cmpid=tpdaily-eml-2014-06-06

126. Willy Blackmore, "Colony Collapse Disorder Is Not What You Think," *Take Part*, 20 June 2014, online at http://www.takepart.com/feature/2014/06/20/what-is-killing-bees?cmpid=tpseries-eml-2014-07-23-bees

127. Richard Coniff, "How Honeybees Use Their Tiny Brains to Do Big Things," *Take Part*, 27 June 2014, online at http://www.takepart.com/article/2014/06/27/how-bees-use-their-tiny-brains-do-big-things?cmpid=tpseries-eml-2014-07-23-bees

128. David O'Brochta, "Genetically-Modified Honey Bees: A Key Technology for Honey Bee Research," *Entomology Today*, 11 July 2014 online at http://entomologytoday.org/2014/06/11/genetically-modified-honey-bees-a-key-technology-for-honey-bee-research/

129. Willy Blackmore, "What Is Killing All the Bees?" *Take Part*, 21 June 2014, online at http://www.takepart.com/feature/2014/06/20/what-is-killing-bees

130. Todd Woody, "Scientists Warn That a Widely Used Pesticide Could Be Worse for the Bees Than DDT," *Take Part*, 24 June 2014, online at http://www.takepart.com/article/2014/06/24/are-neonicotinoids-new-ddt-bees-and-other-wildlife

131. Gregory B. Hladky, "Retailers Selling 'Bee-Friendly' Plants Containing Bee Toxic Pesticides, Report Says," *The Hartford Courant*, 25 June 2014, online at http://articles.courant.com/2014-06-25/news/hc-big-box-bee-pesticides-0626-20140625_1_bees-plants-garden

132. Todd Woody, "Your Bee-Friendly Garden May Be Killing Bees – and Here's What to Do About It," *Take Part*, 25 June 2014, online at http://www.takepart.com/article/2014/06/25/your-bee-friendly-backyard-may-actually-be-killing-bees?cmpid=tpdaily-eml-2014-06-26

133. Peter Power – Photo Gallery: "Ontario's beekeepers launch a campaign against pesticide use," *The Globe and Mail*, 25 June 2014, online at http://www.theglobeandmail.com/report-on-business/ontarios-beekeepers-launch-a-campaign-against-pesticide-use/article19205521/?from=20319629

134. Maryam Henein, "White House Launches Plan to Save the Bees," *Honey Colony*, 26 June 2014, online at http://www.honeycolony.com/article/white-house-plan-save-the-bees/

135. Polly Mosendz, "'Bee-Friendly' Plants Sold at Big Box Stores Are Actually Killing Bees," *The Wire*, 26 June 2014, online at http://www.thewire.com/business/2014/06/bee-friendly-plants-sold-at-big-box-stores-are-actually-killing-bees/373537/

136. Richard Coniff, "How Honeybees Use Their Tiny Brains to Do Big Things," *Take Part*, 27 June 2014, online at http://www.takepart.com/article/2014/06/27/how-bees-use-their-tiny-brains-do-big-things?cmpid=tpseries-eml-2014-07-23-bees

137. Willy Blackmore, "Home Depot Decides Secret Pesticides Probably Don't Belong in Bee-Friendly Plants," *Take Part*, 30 June 2014, online at http://www.takepart.com/article/2014/06/30/home-depot-label-neonics?cmpid=tpdaily-eml-2014-07-01

138. Stephanie Snay, "Beneficial bees help your garden grow," *Angie's List*, 2 July 2014, online at http://www.angieslist.com/articles/beneficial-bees-help-your-garden-grow.htm?cid=SocialLife_20140718_28069246

139. Michael McAuliff, "Americans Are Too Stupid For GMO Labeling, Congressional *Panel Says,*" *The Huffington Post*, 10 July 2014, online at http://www.huffingtonpost.com/2014/07/10/gmo-labels-congress_n_5576255.html

140. Tom Philpott, "Your Almond Habit is Sucking California Dry," *Mother Jones*, 14 July 2014, online at http://www.motherjones.com/tom-philpott/2014/07/your-almond-habit-sucking-califoirnia-dry

141. Todd Woody, "Good News for the Bees: The Government Ends Pesticide Use in Some Wildlife Refuges," *Take Part*, 16 July 2014, online at http://www.takepart.com/article/2014/07/16/good-news-bees-government-bans-pesticide-use-wildlife-refuges?cmpid=tpseries-eml-2014-07-23-bees

142. Diana Yates, "Scientists track gene activity when honey bee do and don't eat honey," *University of Illinois News Bureau*, 17 July 2014, online at http://news.illinois.edu/news/14/0717honey_bee_diet_GeneRobinson.html

143. Tom Philpott, "The EPA Dithers While a Popular Pesticide Threatens Ecosystems," *Mother Jones*, 18 July 2014, online at http://www.motherjones.com/tom-philpott/2014/07/silent-spring-eternal-epa-dithers-while-popular-pesticide-threatens-ecosystems

144. University of Kentucky College of Agriculture, "A World Without Bees," *Take Part*, 23 July 2014, online at http://www.takepart.com/photos/world-without-bees?cmpid=tpseries-eml-2014-07-23-bees

145. David Kirby, "We May Soon Be Living in a World Overrun by Rats," *Take Part*, 28 July 2014, online at http://www.takepart.com/article/2014/07/27/how-great-extinction-wildlife-underway-affects-your-health?cmpid=tpdaily-eml-2014-07-28

146. Damian Carrington, "Bee research tainted by corporate funding, MPs say," *The Guardian*, 28 July 2014, online at http://www.theguardian.com/environment/2014/jul/28/bee-research-funding-pesticides-mps?CMP=twt_gu

147. "Pesticides Linked to Drug-Resistant Fungal Infections in Humans," *Beyond Pesticides*, 29 July 2014, online at http://www.beyondpesticides.org/dailynewsblog/?p=13752

148. "UK Parliament Finds Unacceptable Influence of Pesticide Company Pollinator Research on Regulatory Decisions," *Beyond Pesticides*, 30 July 2014, online at http://www.beyondpesticides.org/dailynewsblog/?p=13763

149. Arjun Walia, "WikiLeaks Cables Reveal U.S. Government Planned to "Retaliate & Cause Pain" on Countries Refusing GMOs," *Collective Evolution*, 30 July 2014, online at http://www.collective-evolution.com/2014/07/30/wikileaks-cables-reveal-u-s-government-planned-to-retaliate-cause-pain-on-countries-refusing-gmos/

150. "National Refuges to Ban GE Crops and Bee-Killing Pesticides," *Beyond Pesticides*, 1 August 2014, online at http://www.beyondpesticides.org/dailynewsblog/?p=13794

151. "House Votes to Roll Back Protections from Pesticides Put in Nation's Waters," *Beyond Pesticides*, 4 August 2014, online at http://www.beyondpesticides.org/dailynewsblog/?p=13801

152. Eric Atkins, "Industry group warns pesticide ban would 'handcuff' farmers," *The Globe and Mail*, 4 August 2014, online

at http://www.theglobeandmail.com/report-on-business/the-battle-over-pesticides/article19909522/

153. "Vermont Law School Becomes First BEE Protective Campus," *Beyond Pesticides*, 11 August 2014, online at http://www.beyondpesticides.org/dailynewsblog/?p=13843

154. Willy Blackmore, "More Midwestern Bees Will Get a Break From Pesticides," *Take Part*, 4 August 2014, online at http://www.takepart.com/article/2014/08/04/minnesota-neonic-ban?cmpid=tpseries-eml-2014-08-15-bees

155. Judy Benson, "Abuzz Over Beekeeping," *The Day*, 17 August 2014, online at http://m.theday.com/article/20140817/NWS01/308179943/1113/mobile&template=mobile

156. Julie Wilson, "Overused fungicides give rise to deadly, resistant fungus threatening humans and crops," *Natural News*, 19 August 2014, online at http://www.naturalnews.com/046517_fungicides_chemical_resistance_fumigation.html?utm_content=bufferb44a0&utm_medium=social&utm_source=facebook.com&utm_campaign=buffer

157. Ocean Robbins, "Huge news for the birds and the bees," *The Food Revolution Network*, 21 August 2014, online at http://foodrevolution.org/blog/birds-and-bees/

158. Todd Woody, "California to Bees: Drop Dead," *Take Part*, 26 August 2014, online at http://www.takepart.com/article/2014/08/26/california-bees-drop-dead?cmpid=tpdaily-eml-2014-08-26

159. Rob Davis, "Oregon Spray Pilot Fined $10,000 for Pesticide Drift that Residents Say Poisoned Them," *Beyond Pesticides*, 26 August 2014, online at http://www.beyondpesticides.org/dailynewsblog/?p=13922

160. Anita Hofschneider, "Federal Court Blocks Local Pesticide and GE Law in Kauai," *Beyond Pesticides*, 27 August 2014, online at http://www.beyondpesticides.org/dailynewsblog/?p=13932

161. Eric Atkins, "Beekeepers file suit against pesticide makers Syngenta and Bayer," *The Globe and Mail*, 3 September 2014, online at http://www.theglobeandmail.com/report-on-business/beekeepers-plan-to-sue-pesticide-makers-over-bee-deaths/article20319629/

162. Tiffany Stecker, "Syngenta asks EPA to raise tolerance level for 'bee-killing' chemical," *E&E Publishing*, 5 September 2014, online at http://www.eenews.net/stories/1060005321

163. Danielle Nierenberg and Maia Reed , "Does Organic Make Food Better for You?" Food Tank, 7 September 2014, online at http://foodtank.com/news/2014/09/organic-produce-higher-in-nutritional-content-than-conventional-produce

164. Tiffany Stecker, "Manufacturer Proposes Increase in Bee-Toxic Pesticide on Crops," *Beyond Pesticides*, 9 September 2014, online at http://www.beyondpesticides.org/dailynewsblog/?p=14016

Editorials

165. "Bee Survival in Europe," *The New York Times*, 25 October 2013, online at http://www.nytimes.com/2013/10/26/opinion/international/bee-survival-in-europe.html?action=click

166. Laura Turner Seydel, "Support the 'Save America's Pollinators Act' – Why We Must Work Together to Save the Bees," *The Huffington Post*, 11 December 2013, online at http://www.huffingtonpost.com/laura-turner-seydel/support-the-save-americas_b_4426904.html

167. Donald E. Williams Jr. and Tara Cook-Littman, "Labelling GMOs Protects People, Environment," *The Hartford Courant*, 21 December 2013, online at http://www.courant.com/news/opinion/hc-op-williams-connecticut-labels-gmo-protects-peo-20131220,0,2779654.story

168. Tom Philpott, "First We Fed Bees High-Fructose Corn Syrup, Now We've Given Them a Killer Virus?" *Mother Jones*,

February 5, 2014, online at http://www.motherjones.com/tom-philpott/2014/02/whats-killing-bees-plot-thickens

169. Alicia Graef, "If We Put Bees on the Endangered List Now, Maybe We Won't Be Screwed Later," *Care2*, 17 May 2014, online at http://www.care2.com/causes/if-we-put-bees-on-the-endangered-list-now-maybe-we-wont-be-screwed-later.html

170. Mark Winston, "Our Bees, Ourselves – Bees and Colony Collapse," *The New York Times*, 14 July 2014, online at http://www.nytimes.com/2014/07/15/opinion/bees-and-colony-collapse.html?_r=0

Bee Art

171. Christopher Jobson and William Eakin, "Artist Aganetha Dyck Collaborates with Bees to Create Sculptures Wrapped in Honeycomb," *Colossal Art & Visual Culture*, 19 February 2014, online at http://www.thisiscolossal.com/2014/02/artist-aganetha-dyck-collaborates-with-bees-to-create-sculptures-wrapped-in-honeycomb/

Books

172. Rachel Carson. SILENT SPRING. New York: Houghton Mifflin Harcourt Publishing Company. 1962. Reprint 2002.

173. Frank R. Stockton. Illustrations by Maurice Sendak. THE BEE-MAN OF ORN. 1964.

174. Sue Hubbell. A BOOK OF BEES. New York: Houghton Mifflin Company. New York, Chicago, San Francisco: Holt, Rinehart and Winston. 1988.

175. Jay Hosler. CLAN APIS. Columbus, Ohio: An Active Synapse Production. 2000-2007.

176. Amos I. Root, Ann Harman, Hachiro Shimanuki, and Kim Flottum. THE ABC & XYZ OF BEE CULTURE: AN ENCYCLOPEDIA PERTAINING TO THE SCIENTIFIC AND PRACTICAL CULTURE OF HONEY BEES. Medina, Ohio: A.I. Root Company. 2007.

177.   Rowan Jacobsen. FRUITLESS FALL: THE COLLAPSE OF THE
       HONEY BEE AND THE COMING AGRICULTURAL CRISIS. New
       York: Bloomsbury U.S.A. 2008.

Online Videos

178.   Matt H. Mayes and Axel Gerdau, "A Disastrous Year for Bees,"
       The New York Times, March 28, 2013, #100000
       http://www.nytimes.com/video/2013/03/28/science/earth/100000
       002143340/a-disastrous-year-for-bees.html?ref=earth
       002143340 This is an online video that runs 2 minutes and 41
       seconds.

179.   Alexis Baden-Mayer, "GMO A Go Go!" *Causes: Stop
       "Natural" Fraud*, January 5, 2014, online at
       https://www.causes.com/posts/819194?auto_prompt_sharing=tru
       e&utm_campaign=user_post_mailer%2Ftrending&utm_content
       =cta_video&utm_medium=email&utm_source=causes&ctag=5e
       f786df5d2fce03c6e19f1cd0f5757351&ctoken=9ffn37bWw4naK
       oapIdHLc10hCqubF-H-nQOQeFbe_GIiCfPriLsMlwny-
       7mYmbnLjUCX8ZaRj-
       Zojt2xaw3UeA%3D%3D&uid=184101159 This is an online
       video that runs 9 minutes and 23 seconds.

180.   Scott Tucker, "The Honey Bee," *Temple University Television*,
       18 June 2013, online at http://templetv.net/shows/expedition-
       new-england/the-honey-bee/ and http://templetv.net/watch-live/
       Scott Tucker finally makes contact with Connecticut's state bee
       keeper Mark Creighton, and not only does Scott get the privilege
       of examining an active bee hive, he gets a step-by-step lesson on
       how to properly approach these insects without ever getting
       stung once. He gets the latest scoop on "Colony Collapse
       Disorder" (CCD) and its likely causes. In addition to the
       physical exam of the hive, Mark delves into the physics and
       chemistry of bees in such a way that we get a real appreciation
       for how much work is required to produce a single drop of
       honey.

181.   Marla Spivak, "Why Bees Are Disappearing," *TEDGlobal*, June
       2013, online at
       http://www.ted.com/talks/marla_spivak_why_bees_are_disappea

ring?utm_source=direct-
on.ted.com&awesm=on.ted.com_h0RiC&utm_medium=on.ted.c
om-facebook-share&utm_content=awesm-
inlinelinkcreator&utm_campaign=ted Spivak explains how bees
go out to get pollen and nectar because they need to eat, and in
so doing provide a valuable service of pollination. She also
describes how, in parts of the world without bees, people are
paid to pollinate by hand with vibrators and paint brushes.

Documentaries

182. *Vanishing of the Bees*. Directed by George Langworthy and
      Maryam Henein, 2009. Narrated by Ellen Page (Hipfuel and
      Hive Mentality Films). This documentary describes Colony
      Collapse Disorder, which is threatening the world bee population
      and with it the future growing capability of fruits, vegetables,
      and flowers – with no explanation or solution – exploring its
      economic, ecological, and political consequences.

183. *Queen of the Sun: What Are the Bees Telling Us?* Directed by
      Taggart Siegel, 2010. Starring Gunther Hauk, Michael Pollan,
      and Vandana Shiva. Queen of the Sun takes viewers on a
      journey through the catastrophic disappearance of bees and the
      mysterious world of the beehive, revealing the dramatic stories
      of beekeepers, scientists and philosophers from around the
      world.

184. *The Queen of Versailles*. Directed by Lauren Greenfield, 2012.
      Starring Jackie and David Siegel, owners of Westgate Resorts,
      and their family as they build the largest and most expensive
      single-family house in the United States, the excessive
      consumption of resources of this family and lack of concern
      about that aspect of their habits, along with the crisis they face
      as the U.S. economy declines.

Movies that Involve Beekeeping

185. *Ulee's Gold*. Directed by Victor Nunez, 1997. Starring Peter
      Fonda, Patricia Richardson, and Christine Dunford. The
      beekeeping operation depicted in this work of fiction shows how
      small beekeeping operations work. This story was created just as

mites were starting to threaten them. It shows Langstroth beehives and construction, a bee swarm capture, and honey extractions.

Honeybee Art and Photography

186. Sam Droege and the USGS Bee Inventory and Monitoring Lab, "Macro Bee Portraits," *Colossal Art & Visual Culture*, 20 December 2013, online at http://www.thisiscolossal.com/2013/12/bee-portraits-sam-droege/

Comic Strips

187. Alex Hallatt, "Ban Neonicotinoids," 6 April 2013, *Arctic Circle*. "Those bees are protesting against dangerous pesticides," says the rabbit to the penguin as some bees try to carry a picket sign.

Bee Journals

http://www.beeculture.com/

http://www.blisshoneybees.org/default.html

http://www.honeycolony.com/

Top Bar Beekeeping
http://top-bar-beekeeping.wikidot.com/

Bee Hive Construction

Top Bar Construction by Dennis Murrell
http://www.beesource.com/resources/elements-of-beekeeping/alternative-hive-designs/top-bar-hive-construction-dennis-murrell/

Beekeepers

Kirk Webster
Champlain Valley Bees and Queens
Box 381
Middlebury, Vermont 05753
(802) 989-5895
(802) 758-2501
No e-mail – use the U.S. Postal Service.
http://kirkwebster.com/

Jim Doan
Doan Family Farms
343 Morton Road
Hamlin, New York 14464
(585) 659-9141
jdoan@rochester.rr.com

Kim Flottum
Honeybee Expert and Bee Culture *Editor*
http://www.motherearthnews.com/biographies/kim-flottum.aspx#axzz30pLSQmQp

Ted and Becky Jones
Jones' Apiaries
55 Wolf Pit Road
Farmington, Connecticut 06032
Phone: (860) 677-9391
Fax: (860) 677-1603
Website: http://jonesapiaries.com/

Dennis Murrell
Wyoming
usbwrangler@juno.com

Tom Theobald
Niwot Honey Farm
P.O. Box 33
Niwot, Colorado 80544-0033
(303) 652-2266
bkpr.tom@indra.com

Steven Ellis
Old Mill Honey Company, L.L.C.
20501 County Road 5
Barrett, Minnesota 56311-1111

Bill Rhodes
Bill Rhodes Honey Co., L.L.C.
38430 Timberlane Drive
Umatilla, Florida 32784-9307
(352) 516-1134
(352) 669-7373
http://www.maryanndesantis.com/wp-content/uploads/2012/03/1110-UmatillaGold.pdf

Peter Roberts
Tall Pines Apiary
6325 81st Street
Vero Beach, Florida 32967
(772) 559-9943
kerr_m@bellsouth.net
tallpineshoney@bellsouth.net

Bee-Keeping Supply Vendors

Betterbee – Beekeepers Serving Beekeepers
8 Meader Road
Greenwich, New York 12834-2734
(800) 632-3379
http://www.betterbee.com/

Brushy Mountain Bee Farm

610 Bethany Church Road
Moravian Falls, North Carolina 28654
(800) BEESWAX/(800) 233-7929
http://www.brushymountainbeefarm.com/

Dadant & Sons
51 South 2nd Street
Hamilton, Illinois 62341
(217) 847-3324
http://www.dadant.com/

Draper's Super Bee Apiaries, Inc.
32 Avonlea Lane
Millerton, Pennsylvania 16936
(800) 233-4273
(570) 537-2381
sales@draperbee.com
http://www.draperbee.com/index.htm

Glenn Apiaries
P.O. Box 2737
Fallbrook, California 92088-2737
The website contains a list of supplier contact data.
http://www.glenn-apiaries.com/bee_supply_companies.html

Kelley Beekeeping – Serving the Beekeeper Since 1924
A Walter T. Kelley Company
Walter T. Kelley
P.O. Box 240
Clarkson, Kentucky 42726
(800) 233-2899
https://www.kelleybees.com/

Mann Lake, Ltd. – We Know Bees
501 1st Street South
Hackensack, Minnesota 56452
(800) 8807694
http://www.mannlakeltd.com/

Maxant Honey Processing Equipment
P.O. Box 454
Ayer, Massachusetts 01432
(978) 722-BEES

(978) 722-0576
http://www.maxantindustries.com/

Miller Bee Supply
496 Yellow Banks Road
North Wilkesboro, North Carolina 28659
(336) 670-2249
http://www.millerbeesupply.com/

New England Beekeeping Supplies, Inc.
Bee-Cause Apiaries and **Carlisle Honey**
10 Louis Avenue
Tyngsboro, Massachusetts 01879
(877) 632-3371
http://www.nebees.com/

Pigeon Mountain Trading Company
General Store and Beekeeping Supplies
106 North Duke Street
LaFayette, Georgia 30728
(706) 638-1491
http://www.pigeonmountaintrading.com/

Sacramento Beekeeping Supplies
2110 X Street
Sacramento, California 95818
(916) 451-2337
http://www.sacramentobeekeeping.com/

Virginia Beekeeping Supply & Andralyn Farm
101 W. Marshall Street
Remington, Virginia 22734
(540) 905-5563
http://www.virginiabeesupply.com/

Vita Europe Limited
Vita House, London Street
Basingstoke, Hants RG21 7PG
United Kingdom
Telephone: +44 (0)1256 473175
Fax: +44 (0)1256 473179
info@vita-europe.com
http://www.vita-europe.com/products/apiguard/

Western Bee Supplies, Inc.
P.O. Box 190, 5
9th Avenue East
Polson, Montana 59860
(406) 883-2918
(800) 548-8440
http://westernbee.com/

Wood's Beekeeping Supply & Academy
690 George Washington Highway
Lincoln, Rhode Island 02865
(401) 305-2355
http://www.woodsbees.com/

Honeybee Associations

American Beekeeping Federation
http://www.abfnet.org/

Bee Natural
http://talkingstick.me/bees/

Bee Source
http://www.beesource.com/

California State Beekeepers Association
http://www.californiastatebeekeepers.com/

Connecticut State Beekeepers Association
http://ctbees.com/

Florida State Beekeepers Association
http://floridabeekeepers.org/

Pennsylvania State Beekeepers Association
http://www.pastatebeekeepers.org/

Russian Honeybee Breeder Association
http://www.russianbreeder.org/

Laws and Regulations

FFDCA – Federal Food, Drug, and Cosmetic Act of 1938
21 U.S.C. 9 §301 et seq.

FIFRA – Federal Insecticide, Fungicide, and Rodenticide Act of 1947
7 U.S.C. §136 et. seq.

FIFRA – Federal Insecticide, Fungicide, and Rodenticide Act of 1947
7 U.S.C. §18 et. seq.
Emergency Exemption from Registrations

ESA – Endangered Species Act of 1973
16 U.S.C. §1531

FQPA – Food Quality Protection Act of 1996
7 U.S.C. §136d, 7 U.S.C. §136a-1, 7 U.S.C. §136w, 7 U.S.C. §136, 7
U.S.C. §136a, 7 U.S.C. §136q

H.R. 2692: Saving America's Pollinators Act of 2013
https://www.govtrack.us/congress/bills/113/hr2692
This is not yet a law. Who knows if and when the U.S. government will
have the sense to actually enact it into law?
Regardless, this is a proposed law, a logical idea…and here is a way to
track it and see how it's doing.

Matthew Porter, "State Preemption Law: The Battle for Control of
Local Democracy," *Pesticides and You*, Fall 2013, online at
http://www.beyondpesticides.org/lawn/activist/documents/StatePreemp
tion.pdf

United States Environmental Protection Agency Data

"What are Biopesticides?"
http://www.epa.gov/pesticides/biopesticides/whatarebiopesticides.htm

U.S. Environmental Protection Agency
Pesticide Emergency Exemptions
"Section 18 of Federal Insecticide, Fungicide, and Rodenticide Act
(FIFRA) authorizes EPA to allow an unregistered use of a pesticide for
a limited time if EPA determines that an emergency condition
exists. The regulations governing Section 18 of FIFRA (found at Title

40 of the Code of Federal Regulations, part 166), define the term "Emergency Condition" as an urgent, non-routine situation that requires the use of a pesticide(s). Such uses are often referred to as "emergency exemptions," "Section 18s," or simply "exemptions.'"
http://www.epa.gov/opprd001/section18/

U.S.D.A. Honey Bee Breeding, Genetics and Physiology Laboratory

Thomas E. Rinderer
Research Leader
Tom.Rinderer@ars.usda.gov
1157 Ben Hur Road
Baton Rouge, Louisiana 70820
U.S.A.
225-767-9281
http://www.ars.usda.gov/Main/site_main.htm?modecode=64-13-30-00

Apiary Inspector

Mark H. Creighton
Connecticut State Apiary Inspector
Lockwood Farm
880 Evergreen Avenue
Hamden, Connecticut 06518
Phone: (203) 974-8618
80-Acre Research Farm – 10 Hives

Databases

National Pesticide Information Center (NPIC)
http://npic.orst.edu/ingred/mfgrdata.htm

National Pesticide Information Retrieval System (NPIRS)
http://ppis.ceris.purdue.edu/
The site offers this advice:
Search for federally active pesticide products using *one* of the following methods: EPA Registration Number, Product Name, Company Name or Active Ingredient. Only a single keyword i.e.,

lemongrass or keyword set i.e., lemon oil, may be used as your search criterion.

Non-Governmental Organizations

Beyond Pesticides
701 E Street, S.E. – Suite 200
Washington, D.C. 20003
Phone: 202-543-5450
http://www.beyondpesticides.org/

Center for Environmental Health
2201 Broadway – Suite 302
Oakland, California 94612
Phone: (510) 655-3900
http://www.ceh.org/

Center for Food Safety
660 Pennsylvania Avenue, S.E. – #302
Washington, D.C. 20003
Phone: 202-547-9359
www.centerforfoodsafety.org/

Pesticide Action Network North America
1611 Telegraph Avenue – Suite 1200
Oakland, California 94612
Phone: 510-788-9020
http://www.panna.org/

Sierra Club
85 Second Street – 2nd Floor
San Francisco, California 94105
Phone: 415-977-5500
http://www.sierraclub.org/

Acknowledgements

There are many people I would like to thank for their help in preparing this book.

One is David D. Haines, Ph.D., for going over scientific details and thus ensuring that I expressed what is happening to the natural world accurately and completely.

Next, my parents, for buying honey on their trip to Florida and putting me in touch with a beekeeper, who lives and operates hives there.

That is not all that my parents have done to assist me. My father, Paul W. Fox, has equipped me with a professional camera. This was very useful in compiling a collection of images to include in this project.

My mother, Carole B.C. Fox, went over the manuscript for this book very carefully and critically, conducting a much-needed edit. As I always say, no one can edit one's own work and hope to spot every error.

Thank you to Xandra Black for sending me lots of fascinating bee art on Facebook.

Thank you very much to Peter Roberts, a beekeeper in Vero Beach, Florida who runs Tall Pines Apiary, for talking to me about his operation. He runs a small, non-traveling apiary that supplies local stores and restaurants. Mr. Roberts also sells his honey, which includes delicious wildflower and tupelo flavors, at a farmers' market in his town.

A local hobbyist beekeeper in West Hartford, Connecticut, Kevin Krebsbach, M.D., was very helpful and willing to share his experience with me. He keeps several hives at a farm called Westmoor Park. He described his operation, which he keeps organic, and explained that his hives are surrounded by a suburban neighborhood. He was kind enough to invite me to visit his hives with my camera, which supplied me with many of the images in this book.

He explained that many homeowners likely use insecticides in their yards, which affect his bees when they forage. He loses over fifty percent of his hives each year, and replaces them with swarms that split off from Farmington, Connecticut apiaries. He also raises queen bees and sells them. He gives his honey away to friends and colleagues.

Thank you to Michael Cavanaugh, a self-described novice beekeeper, for inviting me to photograph his two Langstroth hives in East Longmeadow, Massachusetts. He and his children, Janelle and Aiden, who instigated the family's beekeeping operation out of concern for the environment, showed me every bit of their equipment and demonstrated it. They also described the beekeeping course that they took over the previous winter.

Thanks also to Jane Shriver Coe of Boxford, Massachusetts for describing the beekeeping efforts of her late husband, Thomas D. Coe, to me over the phone. I will always remember his gifts to me of honey from those hives and homemade, seedless red raspberry jam, which his bees made possible. Visiting with him and his wife was one of my favorite parts of going to visit my best friend from college, Elizabeth I. Coe Wheeler.

Her daughter-in-law, Linda Hornstra Coe, was equally forthcoming with details on those hives, which she endeavored to keep going after Thomas Coe's death. She managed it for a few more years before colony collapse disorder set in, leaving the hives empty. I thank her for writing me a comprehensive e-mail about this depressing outcome.

A huge, absolutely delighted thank-you goes to Mark Creighton, Connecticut's Apiary Inspector, for a personal appearance and demonstration of his 10 hives at the Connecticut Agricultural Experiment Station at Lockwood Farm in Hamden, Connecticut.

He was extremely welcoming and forthcoming with bee photographs and a bee photo-op, a detailed discussion of bee, bee viruses, bacteria, parasites, and neonicotinoids, and he showed me and my mother, who edited this manuscript, both varroa mites and how he gets rid of many of them: with confectioner's sugar. The bees eat it off of each other, dislodging the parasites!

Connecticut Apiary Inspector Mark Creighton shaking powdered sugar into one of his hives, and a worker bee walking around the hive, dusted with it. He calls them "ghost bees".

We had a wonderfully fun and instructive afternoon with him, and thoroughly enjoyed meeting him.

About the Author

Stephanie C. Fox, J.D. is a historian, writer, and editor. She is a graduate of William Smith College and the University of Connecticut School of Law. Ms. Fox has written several books on a variety of topics, including the effects of human overpopulation on the environment, Asperger's, and travel to Kuwait and Hawai'i.

She runs an editing service called *QueenBeeEdit*, which caters to politicians, scientists, and others. Her imprint is *QueenBeeBooks*.

Her areas of interest include – but are not limited to – history, herstory, biographies, women's studies, science fiction, dystopian fiction, human overpopulation, ecosystems collapse, environmental law, international relations, Asperger's, and cats.

Her website may be viewed at:

www.queenbeeedit.com

About the Illustrator

Lauren Jane Leipold is native to in the Chicago area, but currently operates out of California. She studied fine art at Cornell College and the Institute of Art. She focused on multiple media, including: pen, pencil, pastel, chalk, acrylic and oil paint, watercolor, and ink and turpentine.

As the owner of her own custom works company, she offers paintings, drawings, photographic logos, illustrations, portraits, and landscape pieces.

To view a portfolio of her work, please visit:

www.LJArtExpressions.com
Instagram: lowren89
Twitter: @LoWren89
Facebook: Lauren Jane Leipold

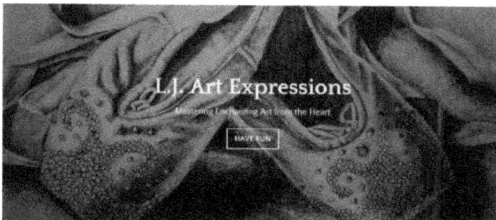

160

www.ingramcontent.com/pod-product-compliance
Lightning Source LLC
Chambersburg PA
CBHW041214030426
42336CB00023B/3345